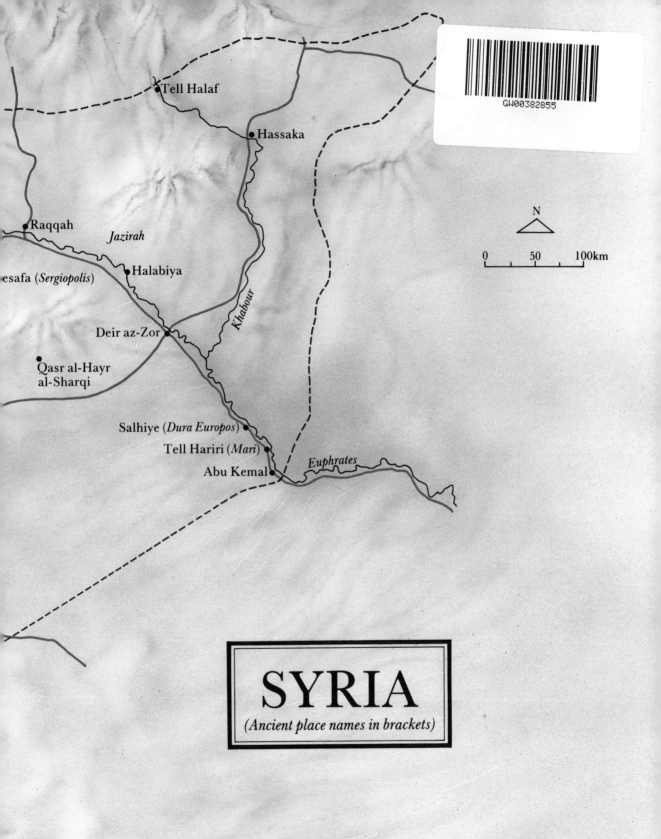

Tell Halaf

Hassaka

Raqqah

Jazirah

esafa (*Sergiopolis*)

Halabiya

Khabour

Deir az-Zor

Qasr al-Hayr
al-Sharqi

Salhiye (*Dura Europos*)

Tell Hariri (*Mari*)

Abu Kemal

Euphrates

N

0   50   100km

SYRIA

(Ancient place names in brackets)

SYRIA IN VIEW

Early morning, Palmyra.

SYRIA·IN·VIEW

Text and photographs
by MICHAEL JENNER

Longman

Shepherd near Krak des Chevaliers.

Longman Group UK Limited,
Longman House, Burnt Mill, Harlow,
Essex CM20 2JE, England
and Associated Companies throughout the world.

First published 1986

British Library Cataloguing in Publication Data
Jenner, Michael, 1946–
Syria in view.
1. Syria – History
I. Title
956.91 DS95

ISBN 0-582-78397-6

Set in 11/14 Lasercomp Baskerville

Printed in Hong Kong
by Longman Group (FE) Ltd

Contents

		page
Acknowledgements		xvi
Introduction		xvii
CHAPTER ONE	Uncovering the Early Past	1
CHAPTER TWO	Aramaeans, Phoenicians, Greeks and Romans	15
CHAPTER THREE	The Cradle of Christianity	33
PICTURE SECTION	The Monuments of Syria	47
CHAPTER FOUR	The Umayyads and the Dawn of Islam	79
CHAPTER FIVE	The Legacy of the Crusades	95
CHAPTER SIX	Damascus and Aleppo	109
A note on the transliteration of Arabic proper names		125
Selected further reading		126
Index		140

Sheep grazing in the Great Syrian Desert.

Halabiya on the Euphrates.

Young shepherd near St Simeon's Church (above).

Sheep by the Euphrates (left).

Young girl at Al-Bara.

Woman of the Jazirah.

Shepherd of the desert.

Druze couple in the Hauran.

Women in the fields in the Jazirah.

Women in the fields in the Jazirah.

Acknowledgements

The research and photography for this book were carried out over a number of visits to Syria made possible thanks to the unfailing support of the Minister of Tourism, HE Naoras El Daker. His far-sighted commitment to promoting awareness of Syria's heritage was a great encouragement. A debt of gratitude is also due to many other individuals at the Ministry of Tourism such as Mouafak El Khani, Abdul Hadi Namani, Ihsan Chichakli, Sahar Nassour, Elias Boulad and especially to M. Usama Kuwatli for his painstaking advice on the manuscript. At the Department of Antiquities and Museums, valuable assistance was received from Dr Afif Bahnassi, Dr Adnan Bounni, Kassem Toueir, Adnan Jundi, M. Wahid Khayta and others too numerous to mention. Special thanks are due to Günter Schachtner, both in his capacity as Director General of Meridien Hotels in Syria as well as Special Councillor to the Ministry of Tourism. The hospitality and kindness of the directors and staff at the Meridien hotels in Latakia, Palmyra and Damascus is gratefully acknowledged. The Mazloumian family at the Baron Hotel in Aleppo was always welcoming and did much to acquaint me with the attractions of northern Syria. Much useful advice and guidance was also given by Georges Antaki, Moussa Chalhoub, Dr Abdel Aziz Alloun, Abdallah Hadjar, and Jim Dunn and Linda Addison of Travel Press Service Ltd. Special thanks to Andy Smart for his creative editing. Finally, thanks are due also to Syrianair and to my drivers Yasser Karbouj and Mouafak Toto, who became firm friends in the course of our travels. Their care and companionship throughout our journeys to all parts of the country helped me to appreciate the warmth and good humour of the Syrian people.

Michael Jenner, London 1985

Introduction

The succession of different civilisations in Syria, which are the subject of this book, have made the Syrian Arab Republic the most widely endowed country in a region of tremendous archaeological interest. Syria's cultural heritage is amazingly diverse as well as awesomely ancient. Yet it is only in this century that an idea of its remote past has been obtained and that an authentic Syrian Arab identity has been discovered amidst the evidence of so many neighbouring cultures on Syrian soil. This book is an attempt both to illustrate the almost bewildering abundance of civilisation in Syria through the ages, and at the same time to refer to the achievements of some of the countless archaeologists and historians, to whose efforts this work is greatly indebted.

The focus of interest shifts gradually from the investigation and excavation of the early sites such as Mari, Ebla and Ugarit to the Greco-Roman period of Palmyra and Bosra. The sites of early Christianity, notably St Simeon's Church and the 'Dead Cities', then make a brief appearance on the Syrian stage before the dazzling world of the Umayyad caliphate in Damascus establishes Syria as the centre of the expanding Islamic community. The narrative continues with the ambivalent architectural legacy of the Crusades and a rapid review of Aleppo and Damascus which contain the cultural relics of so many chapters of Syrian history. The colour photographs in the centre of the book illustrate the main theme of the succession of civilisations through the ages, while the pictures at the beginning and the end of the book attempt to provide an idea of the physical and human dimension of the country. For it is surely a mistake to see Syria as a vast open-air museum; the archaeology of the country is fascinating but the real heritage must include the people themselves, whose ancestors created the civilisations whose remains we admire today.

Syria has often been described as the crossroads of Near Eastern civilisation, as if to suggest that the country was just an empty space on the junction of routes taken by foreign forces. Certainly, it is true that Syria has always attracted the attentions of the entire Near East in the course of her long and eventful history, but as a place to settle permanently the lands of the Fertile Crescent have exercised a constant pull on the inhabitants of the desert. From the time of the Akkadians, Amorites and Canaanites in the third millennium BC, to that of the Aramaeans in the second, and culminating with the Arab Muslim conquests of the seventh century AD, the assimilation of settlers from the Arabian peninsula has been the leitmotif of Syria's ethnic evolution. The resulting Syrian Arab identity has also been enriched by a series of incursions from north, east and west, so that Syria today can be described not so much as a crossroads but as a lasting meeting-place of the peoples and cultures of the Near East.

Civilisation in Syria thus comprises numerous elements, both home-grown as well as imported from all the cultures of the Near East. Given the multitude of influences exerted on the country it is not surprising that Syria is today a multi-faceted experience, a sort of cultural kaleidoscope. It is best to leave the unravelling of the various parts of the Syrian story until the mind has come to grips with the sheer weight and depth of past civilisations which are represented here. For Syria is more than the sum of her monuments; and the essence of the country would appear to reside partly in the carefree and generous manner in which the vestiges of so many ancient cultures are literally strewn about the landscape, often in mysterious interaction with the world of the twentieth century.

CHAPTER ONE

Uncovering the Early Past

The archaeological exploration of ancient Syria began in fairly recent times when in 1928 a peasant ploughing his field at Ras Shamra on the Mediterranean coast unearthed some flat stones which concealed an underground vault. The following year excavation of the site was commenced under the leadership of the Frenchman M. Claude Schaeffer, and gradually the old Canaanite city of Ugarit emerged into the light of day. During the course of the excavations between 1929 and 1939 a number of tablets were discovered which provided an historical record to document the archaeological finds. It was not until 1948, however, when digging was resumed after the Second World War, that the most spectacular discovery was made, namely the archives of the royal palace. It is to this remarkable collection of tablets that we owe most of our knowledge of Ugarit's flourishing ancient civilisation.

The archaeological evidence pointed to the Canaanites as the main element of the population of Ugarit from as early as the beginning of the second millennium, and trading links with Egypt, Crete, Mycenia and Cyprus are all well attested. But it was with the deciphering of the tablets, which refer to the fourteenth and thirteenth centuries BC, that the life of Ugarit came properly into focus.

A great variety of subjects are covered by the tablets, ranging from personal letters, inventories, commercial matters, legal procedures and international politics to religious ritual and magic. With few exceptions, all the texts of the Ugarit tablets employ the cuneiform system of shaping characters by the use of wedge-shaped strokes, but the languages expressed are several and each appears to have been used for a different subject. Thus we find in the main that Akkadian served for international affairs, Hurrian for religious ritual, Sumerian for mythology and Canaanite for more general use. Although Canaanite was the most commonly spoken tongue there were doubtless a number of separate linguistic groups in a maritime trading city such as Ugarit, and this probably accounts for the most genial invention of the scribes of Ugarit, namely the world's first phonetic alphabet. Faced with the complexities of a polyglot society the problems of communication were greatly eased by this new system of thirty letters, each representing a specific sound. The old method of using hundreds of separate characters to represent entire syllables was thus replaced by a system vastly more convenient. The Canaanite language of Ugarit, known simply as Ugaritic, was not destined to become the lingua franca of the region, but the Ugaritic alphabet was eventually passed on to all Semitic and Indo-European languages. The phonetic alphabet was relayed by the Phoenicians to the Greeks and Romans, and via Aramaic it found its way into Arabic and Hebrew. This breakthrough in communications, as revolutionary in its day as the microchip today, was the inspiration of an anonymous Ugaritic scribe of the fourteenth century BC.

The historical background revealed by the texts of Ugarit confirms the conflict between the two superpowers of the time, the Egyptians and the Hittites. For the most part Ugarit was subject to the Hittites in Carchemish but it asserted its own independence from time to time. Relations with Egypt were evidently of fundamental importance, for one of the imposing homes of Ugarit is now known as the house of the Egyptian ambassador, a person who apparently combined his diplomatic functions with a variety of private business activities. There is correspondence with the city of Qaddesh* in central Syria where in about 1300 BC the Egyptian army under Ramses II met the Hittites in battle. Despite Egyptian claims of a great victory the battle failed to halt the gradual decline of Egyptian power in Syria. However, by the end of the thirteenth century BC, the power of the Hittites in Ugarit had also waned.

It was possibly due to the resulting political vacuum that the Sea Peoples, an obscure mixture of marauders from Asia Minor and the Aegean area, met with little resistance when they fell upon the coastal cities of the eastern Mediterranean. Between 1180 and 1175 BC Ugarit was devastated by a group of these Sea Peoples that included the Philistines, who settled permanently in Syria and

---

*The site of Qaddesh known as Tell Nebi Mend is located to the south of Homs.

gave their name to the entire region of Palestine. It is thought that the site of Ugarit remained unoccupied throughout the next six centuries, playing no part in the flourishing Phoenician civilisation of city-states which emerged after 1200 BC some distance away to the south. Thus was the life of Ugarit extinguished, but its major contribution to world culture survived: the alphabet was further developed by the Phoenicians, whose talent for international commerce turned it to immediate and profitable use.

Ugarit is significant in other ways. Prior to the discovery of the Ugaritic archives practically the only source of information about Canaanite culture and religion was the Old Testament. It is no surprise that the Hebrews, who were convinced of their divine mission to inhabit the land of Canaan as well as of the truth of their Yahweh worship, portrayed the Canaanite Baal as a caricature of heathen idolatry. Through the texts of Ugarit emerges a subtler and more human image of this ancient religion. In the group of poems discovered in the 'House of the High Priest', which have come to be known as the cycle of Baal, we encounter the divine pantheon of the Canaanites and the quintessential mythology of their religious beliefs.

There is El, the supreme god, who in the texts is called 'merciful and generous', 'the creator of the creatures' and 'the father of the years'. Ashirat is the consort of El: she is the mother-goddess who created the other gods. Baal is the son of El, often called the 'rider of the clouds', who is the god of thunder and rain and the master of the earth. Anat, the daughter of El and the sister of Baal, is the goddess of life and fertility. The cycle of Baal tells of the death of Baal at the hands of treacherous Mot, who is the personification of death, and of Baal's triumphant return to life. This parable of life, death and rebirth is thought to be a symbol of the summer drought and the apparent death of all vegetation, followed by the autumn rains bringing back fertility to the earth. Adonis, Ishtar and Astarte can all be traced back to this Canaanite fertility myth; and of course the idea of death and rebirth also became a vital part of Christian belief.

The poems of Ugarit demonstrate a highly evolved literary style which yet retains the authentic simplicity of expression characteristic of ancient legends. Anat's supplication to El is often quoted in this respect:

> 'Your word, O El, is wise.
> Your wisdom is eternal.
> Life is the gift of your word.'

There is the moving lament of the sick man who has come close to death:

> 'I lie awake all night,
> Even in my dreams
> The grave pursues me still
> Pain has me as its prey . . .
> My tears serve me as food.'

There are philosophical reflections in verse which anticipate the literature of much more recent times:

> 'Where are those kings, those great kings of yesteryear?
> They aren't being born any more.'

> 'The hand cannot measure the distance of the sky.
> No one knows how deep is the earth . . .'

> 'Men do not even know what they themselves do.
> The meaning of their nights and days is with the gods.'

Clearly, Ugarit was a sophisticated centre of ancient civilisation with a cultural awareness, belying the accepted wisdom that the peoples of remote antiquity were but the primitive prelude to the glorious achievements of mankind's later development. It would appear from the texts of Ugarit that certain basic insights into the human predicament – as well as certain beliefs – have been with man for at least as long as he has been able to express himself in writing.

Although the texts and the items of statuary have been removed from Ugarit to the Louvre and to the National Museum in Damascus, the site itself is still impressive enough. Built of stone, Ugarit's palaces, libraries, houses, burial chambers and streets have survived the years in better condition than the mud-brick cities of Mesopotamia. The coastal site of the city, with its adjacent port still discernible, suggests a thriving trade encompassing the entire eastern Mediterranean region. The narrow gate of Ugarit, through which the population withdrew in times of trouble, tells of the need for constant vigilance. But, after more than 40 seasons of excavation, only about a quarter of the site has been explored, so Ugarit has still many secrets to reveal. However, the information already gathered establishes Ugarit's leading commercial and cultural role in the Near East of the second half of the second millennium BC, and possibly even earlier. The discovery of Ugarit in this century led to a fundamental re-appraisal of the original inhabitants of Syria and to a new understanding of the country's most ancient history.

In 1933 – only five years after the accidental discovery at Ras Shamra which brought Ugarit to the attention of the archaeologists – a similar episode occurred far away on the eastern flank of Syria. A group of Bedouin were digging in the mound known as Tell Hariri, on the banks of the Euphrates, for a stone appropriate for the grave of a deceased fellow tribesman. Just beneath the surface they came across a headless statue. The news was relayed to Lieutenant Cabane, who represented the French authorities* in the small township of Abu Kemal. The report was investigated and confirmed, and barely a month later the Curator of Oriental Antiquities at the Louvre in Paris was setting things in motion for a proper excavation of the site, under the leadership of Professor André Parrot. Work started on 14 December 1933 and already in January 1934 the Temple of Ishtar was discovered. It contained a statuette inscribed with the name of Lamgi-Mari, King of Mari. The identification of Tell Hariri as Mari was to receive ample confirmation: this was one of the kingdoms mentioned on the Sumerian king-list, which refers to Mari as the seat of the Tenth Dynasty after the Flood. The identification of Mari as the most westerly outpost of Sumerian culture was a significant extension of the previously accepted geographical frontiers of that early civilisation based in southern Mesopotamia. Entire chapters of history, relating not only to the Sumerians but also to the law-giver Hammurabi, the famous King of Babylon at the beginning of the second millennium BC, were awaiting the excavator's spade beneath the mound of Tell Hariri.

Except for the period 1939–51 excavations at Mari have been conducted every year since 1933. Yet such is the size of the site (1000 by 600 metres) that less than half of the total area has been investigated. Nor has it proved possible to determine exactly to what level the layers of occupation descend. According to André Parrot in his book *Mari, Capitale Fabuleuse* (1974), each time that a vertical probe was commenced in order to trace the site's history down to virgin soil, such important discoveries were made that horizontal digging had to be resumed. Available evidence confirmed occupation in the fourth millennium BC, but Parrot did not anticipate any habitation beyond the fifth millennium in

---

*This was the period of the French Mandate imposed by the European powers after the First World War.

spite of the fact that some four metres at the bottom of the tell remained to be explored. The real significance of Mari was to be located in two periods of occupation, in the third and second millennia BC respectively.

The strategic importance of Mari in the third millennium BC was due to its key position as a relay point between the Sumerian settlements of the lower Meso-potamian region and Syria; the latter supplied Sumer with the building materials of timber and stone, unavailable in the delta area. Silver, lead and copper – the latter essential to the development of the culture of the Bronze Age – were also transported to Sumer via Mari. Diplomacy followed in the footsteps of trade: the cache of precious objects discovered at Mari and known as the Treasures of Ur bear witness to a diplomatic mission sent by the first king of the First Dynasty of Ur, around 2500 BC. Commerce was certainly the life-blood of Mari but the works of art which have been unearthed demonstrate that third-millennium Mari was much more than a river-bank trading colony of the Sumerians.

Although the evidence is mainly subjective, both archaeologists and art historians concur that the statues and murals of Mari represent a subtle but extremely significant mutation of Sumerian style through Semitic inspiration. André Parrot describes the sculptures as the work of skilled craftsmen, who had softened and refined the essentially hard models which they were given to interpret. His conclusion is instinctive rather than scientific: 'The original Sumerian culture evolved in Mari within a Semitic environment'. Taking the famous example of the embracing couple – unfortunately headless – Parrot declares, 'Sumerian culture would never have expressed in such a sensitive manner the emotion of a man and a woman holding one another'. Similarly, the statue of the king's favourite singer, Ur-Nina (c2400 BC), and the vast panels of figurative inlay are put forward as illustrations of the Semitic artists' inspired re-interpretation of Sumerian originals.

Who were these Semites in Mari in the middle of the third millennium BC? The histories of the Near East all refer to a large-scale migration of Semitic nomads into the Fertile Crescent at about this time. The Amorites, who settled along the Euphrates, and the Canaanites, who headed west to the coastal region, both trace their roots to this one broad migration from the deserts of Arabia. But if this chronology is correct, is it possible that the Semitic population of Mari achieved the transition from desert nomads to urban dwellers of such high cultural skill within the space of a generation? Or had they been part of an earlier migration along with the Akkadians and ancient Eblaites? Here we are in the realm of conjecture, but the previously accepted dating of the first migration of the Semitic peoples as the middle of the third millennium BC, i.e., that of the Amorites, appears increasingly doubtful.

Likewise, the circumstances surrounding the destruction of Mari's third-millennium civilisation are increasingly subject to careful re-examination. Sargon of Akkad, who ruled in Mesopotamia between c2334 and 2279 BC, had generally been regarded as the culprit. But although he certainly passed through Mari on his famous campaign which took him 'as far as the forests of the cedars and the mountains of silver', historians are beginning to suspect the hand of the Eblaites, who were the commercial rivals of the people of Mari. Be that as it may, Mari's destruction around 2350 BC ushered in a long period of relative decline before the city was to revive once more under the kings of the Amorite dynasty. Mari's second golden age – as witnessed by the archaeological remains of the second millennium BC – commenced around 1900 BC and lasted until about 1750 BC, when the city was again and finally destroyed.

To this brief period of 150 years belong the two most dramatic discoveries at Mari: the palace of Zimri-Lim and the state archives. The palace was found to contain more than 300 rooms and occupied an area measuring some 200 by 120 metres. In all probability this was the largest palace of its time and accordingly its reputation was widespread. This is confirmed by a letter to Zimri-Lim from the King of Yamhad (Aleppo), informing him of the visit of a servant of the King of Ugarit who had heard of the splendour of the royal residence in Mari and had expressed the desire to see it for himself. When the palace was excavated it was discovered that most of the statues had been taken; but one in basalt – of Ishtup-Ilum, who governed Mari in the nineteenth century BC – remained to illustrate the brutal contrast between the new Amorite rulers of Mari and their predecessors of the third millennium BC. Ishtup-Ilum's powerful arms and torso have the predatory quality of the born warrior; the tough mask-like face, with its uncompromising lips, stares through blank emotionless eyes. Another famous statue – dated a century later – is that of the goddess with the flowing vase. Here we encounter feminine grace and aristocratic beauty, the opposite end of the Amorite cultural spectrum. Further examples of the art of the Amorites were provided by the fresco paintings, originally enormous compositions which now survive in small fragments in the Louvre in Paris.

The palace of Zimri-Lim also revealed many details of domestic life at the time. Heated bathrooms, latrines, and kitchens with ovens complete with pots and dishes – all contained within the overall structure of mud-brick – testify to the more basic attainments of building technology. The plumbing arrangements at the palace were discovered still to be in working order some 4000 years after they were originally installed: when a torrential rainstorm flooded the site during the excavations the old system of brick gutters and clay pipes lined with bitumen provided speedy and effective drainage. However, the real treasure concealed in the palace of Zimri-Lim was not the plumbing but the state archives.

The first 300 tablets came to light in February 1935 and since then the number has grown to over 20,000. The Belgian professor Georges Dossin was entrusted with the monumental task of deciphering them and gradually a whole new set of facts emerged which, according to André Parrot, 'brought about a complete revision of the historical dating of the ancient Near East' and provided more than 500 new place names, 'enough to redraw or even draw up the geographical map of the ancient world'. Most of the tablets relate to the reign of Zimri-Lim, and his correspondence with provincial governors reveals much of the everyday reality of public administration. Customs dues, the repair of canals, the provision of delicacies for the royal table, even the despatch of a caged lion, all are documented in the tablets of Mari. There are some touchingly human items too, as for example in a letter from a queen identified as Shibtu to her absent husband: 'May my lord beat his enemies and may my master return to Mari safe and sound with joy in his heart . . . all is well at the palace; the little girls are fine; let my lord's heart not feel disquieted . . .'

Ironically, the most interesting tablets, from the historical point of view, relate to Hammurabi, the destroyer of Mari. In fact, the archives of Mari contain more information about the city of Babylon under this famous law-giver than has been revealed by the evidence originating from Babylon itself. The tablets lay bare the cynical power politics of Hammurabi, who turned on his old ally Zimri-Lim when he judged the moment opportune to extend his sway, and defeated him in battle in 1759 BC. Evidently, this was a shrewd move, for Hammurabi's reign saw the beginning of more than 1000 years of Babylonian dominance over Mesopotamia. This was the time of individual city-states, each trying to survive through diplomatic alliances against the threat of violence and aggression. But diplomacy was to no avail; Hammurabi's destruction of Mari brought a total eclipse to the brilliant civilisation of the court of Zimri-Lim. Despite scattered traces of later Assyrian and Babylonian occupation, by the time the Seleucids arrived on the scene at the end of the fourth century BC Mari was little more than a village. Indeed, the Macedonians of Seleucus I founded an entirely new town on the banks of the Euphrates only a short distance away.

While the excavations at Mari and Ugarit held centre-stage from the 1930s until the 1960s, attention was slowly turning to the remote, prehistoric occupation of Syria. In 1937 and 1938, Max Mallowan's expeditions at Tell Brak, a site on a tributary of the river Khabour forty-three kilometres north of Hassaka, brought to light evidence of sixth-millennium occupation, namely Tell Halaf ware, as well as the mysterious Temple of the Eyes from the second half of the fourth millennium BC. Now the prehistory of Syria was destined to challenge the next generation of archaeologists.

This did not mean, however, that the discoveries made at Ugarit and Mari had satisfied academic curiosity about the history of Syria in the third and second millennia BC. In fact, the most spectacular archaeological evidence of Syria's early history was not excavated until the 1960s and 1970s. Professor Paolo Matthiae of the University of Rome, who first visited Syria in 1964, was not impressed by the great archaeological achievements of his predecessors. Writing in 1977, in his account of his own excavations at Tell Mardikh (*Ebla: An Empire Rediscovered*), Matthiae looked back to the state of archaeology in Syria in 1940: 'It had its moments of brilliant illumination but on the whole left broad areas of thick shade in the cultures of the Old Syrian Period, and scarcely allowed even a glimpse of the great civilisations of the Protosyrian Period.'

Matthiae was at pains to point out the fundamental difference between his structured approach and the haphazard discoveries which occasioned previous excavations: 'It is no longer a matter of isolated cultural episodes emerging from the obscurity of an almost total lack of evidence, but of whole environments brought to light and defined by historical situations which can be identified in space and time.' Tell Mardikh, an imposing mound set in open countryside fifty-five kilometres south of Aleppo, was chosen according to Matthiae because: 'It seemed likely to yield information not only of the immediate antecedents . . . of the period of the Amorite dynasties . . . but also of the more remote and obscure origins of city culture in Syria'. It should be observed that Matthiae was writing *after* making the discoveries which provided answers to the questions. However, his approach to the interpretation of Tell Mardikh confirms his overwhelming ambition to illuminate the broad development of third-millennium Syrian history and culture rather than provide spectacular but isolated finds. What he envisaged at Tell Mardikh was to give 'a total unified account of its successive settlements'. This solidly scientific approach was, however, rewarded by the discovery of Ebla, the greatest commercial and military power in northern Syria during the second half of the third millennium BC, whose state archives shed light on a dark but important period of Syrian culture.

The dig did not meet with immediate success, and by 1968 there was still nothing outstanding to report. Horst Klengel in his *Art of Ancient Syria* (1972) wrote that Tell Mardikh 'cannot compare in importance with Mari or Ugarit', but he concluded his brief description: 'Diggings at Tell Mardikh are only beginning, but the work done so far indicates that much can still be expected.' Possibly the discovery at the end of the fourth season of an inscription mentioning Ebla was the reason for his cautious optimism. In the event, it was not until 1974 that the first tablets – forty-two in number – were unearthed. They contained cuneiform inscriptions both in Sumerian and in a hitherto unknown Semitic language which was classified as 'Palaeo-Canaanite'. However, the dating of the state archives to the period 2400 to 2250 BC raised some revolutionary speculation. It was previously held that, with the exception of Akkadian in northern Syria, there had been no speakers of any Semitic languages prior to the arrival of the Canaanites at the end of the third millennium BC. Indeed, it was widely believed that the inhabitants of Syria at this time were probably not Semites at all. Further study of the language showed it to be closely related to Akkadian, but nonetheless distinct enough from that and later Semitic dialects to merit separate designation as Eblaite. Then, in 1975, an entire library of some 15,000 tablets was uncovered, providing an abundance of historical material.

The characters of the Ebla texts are in the style of classical Mesopotamian cuneiform which had evolved at the end of fourth-millennium Sumer as the language of administration of its first urban centres. Ebla was geographically the most distant place from Sumer where examples of classical Sumerian cuneiform script had been found. However, the script of the Ebla texts was used to express the Semitic tongue now known as Eblaite, which would suggest that Ebla must have been an important city culture in its own right.

From the texts have emerged some fascinating details of that city culture. Commerce appears to have been the main pre-occupation of the people of Ebla. The city controlled the supplies of timber from the coastal hills of Syria as well as metals from Anatolia, both essential to the developing technology of Mesopotamia. Accordingly, the large majority of the tablets so far examined deal with routine matters of commerce and consist of ledgers and inventories. There is evidence that Mari was paying tribute to Ebla and that Ebla was able to impose a commercial treaty on Assur. There is mention of textile exports organised by the state itself to an astounding array of client cities such as Ugarit, Byblos, Kish,

Mari, Assur, Jerusalem and Damascus. Other products of Ebla included fine furniture, tools, weapons and ornaments. This activity required an enormous bureaucracy of some 12,000, as attested by one tablet; this number was drawn from a trading area of 260,000 based on a city proper of 22,400 inhabitants.

In addition to business Ebla seems to have achieved fame as a centre of learning. A school for scribes attracted students from many other cities and the discovery of syllabaries in Eblaite and Sumerian has permitted philologists to understand how Sumerian was expressed by foreigners at a time when it was still a living language. Word-lists of Sumerian and Eblaite arranged in acrophonic order can be regarded as the earliest dictionaries known to history, and there is even a reference to some scribes from Mari attending an academic conference in Ebla.

Central to Matthiae's investigation of the cultural sequences of Ebla was a close study of the architecture and planning of the city. In particular, it was the royal palace which exercised his powers of structural analysis. He found it to be 'a unique monument ... distinct from the Mesopotamian tradition of organic planning on a linear method ... the Palace and Acropolis join up with the residential quarters of Ebla whereas the Mesopotamian palace is by definition self-sufficient, an interruption in the city texture clustering thickly around it'. Matthiae concluded that the art and architecture of the royal palace, 'while manifesting expressions of a peculiarly Syrian higher culture, distinct from the contemporary Mesopotamian culture, shared in a more general unity which still had its great traditional centres in the cities of Sumer and Akkad'. In other words, Ebla injected its own native genius into the mould of Mesopotamian culture and thereby established a new means of expression – typically Syrian in style – which was to be its lasting cultural legacy. This formative period – which Matthiae calls the Mature Protosyrian – was the time when Ebla began to develop and distribute its own authentic store of images. Thus Matthiae boldly called into question the once fashionable argument that art in Syria was no more than the endless borrowing of images from abroad.

The merchants of Ebla themselves might be rather surprised to find their cultural achievements so highly appraised. Indeed, the history of Ebla in the third millennium BC points less to the evolution of artistic style than to military exploits in support of trade. Campaigns were waged against Mari and – as we have seen – it is quite possible that Ebla was responsible for the destruction of that city around 2350 BC. Ebla suffered in turn a similar fate in 2250 BC – probably at the hands of the Akkadians under Naram-Sin – and this marks the end of the period of the state archives as well as of Matthiae's Mature Protosyrian. It is perhaps a sign of the city's vitality at the time that it was immediately rebuilt and that there are no signs of any real break in cultural development.

It is uncertain whether Ebla was able to resume the leading political role it had previously played but it seems unlikely, in view of the late third-millennium incursions of the Amorites into northern Syria, which probably caused a severe disruption of the trading links on which Ebla depended. Around 2000 BC Ebla was destroyed once again, this time by the Amorites who – according to the archaeological evidence – must have caused the city to be rebuilt. It appears that Ebla quickly re-assumed an important economic role in the new era of the Amorite kingdoms and lasted until about 1800 BC when it fell under the sway of Yamhad (Aleppo). The final eclipse of the resplendent merchant-state was at the hands of the Hittites who, in the course of their campaign against Yamhad, also annihilated its most powerful vassals. This destruction occurred in about 1650 BC, since when there has been only partial and sporadic habitation on the site; the most recent occupants were apparently a group of stylite monks at some time between the third and the seventh centuries AD.

The lessons to be learned from the excavations at Tell Mardikh were initially clouded by a bitter controversy. The occurrence of certain names similar and identical to names which appear in the Old Testament triggered off a series of popular articles concerned more with the question of the historicity of the Bible than with the historical facts of Ebla. In view of the tendency, still common in the West, to view the entire development of the Near East in terms of the Bible, it is as well to recall Professor Matthiae's reply to the proponents of biblical archaeology: 'The tablets [of Ebla] cover a period a thousand years before Abraham, and a thousand years, even in the fourth millennium before Christ, was a very, very long time. They tell us much, but what they don't tell us – what they can't tell us – is whether the Bible is true or not. They have nothing to do with the Bible, or at least not directly, and what we have here is not a biblical expedition. If we have tablets with legends similar to those of the Bible it means only that such legends existed round here long before the Bible.'

Meanwhile, archaeological attention in Syria had been shifting to periods much earlier than Ebla. In 1969 a team of German archaeologists began excavating at Habuba Kabira on the upper Euphrates and discovered a settlement over 1000 metres in length sheltering behind a massive wall with a stoutly defensive gate. The place was identified – through pottery and brick types – to be culturally a direct relation of Uruk and thus datable to the fourth millennium

BC. The relationship with Uruk also raised the strong probability that Habuba Kabira was in fact a town founded from southern Mesopotamia in order to control trade. Thus, at a stroke, the frontiers of Syria's involvement in international commerce and its communication with a literate culture were pushed back another thousand years.

The excavation at Habuba Kabira was conducted in some haste, for that stretch of the Euphrates – just above the present-day town of Thawra – was about to be submerged beneath the dammed waters of Lake Assad. The area to be affected was the scene of intense archaeological rescue activity in the 1960s. Among the many sites which were investigated at this time, Mureybet yielded the very earliest pottery samples found in Syria which have been dated to around 8000 BC. The town consisted of a mixture of rectangular and round houses, one of the latter decorated with geometric designs, the earliest examples of mural patterns.

Mureybet also revealed significant evidence about the process of sedentarisation. It had been often claimed that it was the need or desire to cultivate food that led to the first permanently occupied human settlements. Mureybet – and other sites such as Buqras – have now shown that the transition to a sedentary life in fact preceded the shift from hunting and gathering to farming and animal husbandry. However, later phases of occupation at Mureybet (8000–7600 BC) do indicate a heavy reliance on a cereal diet. Was the upper Euphrates region under cultivation at that time? The question must remain open and the exact circumstances of that important step towards the organised production of food are still unclear. Certainly, the sixth millennium BC witnessed the spread of rainfed agriculture in the Near East, and it is increasingly to northern Syria that archaeologists are now looking in order to determine more precisely where, how and when this essential step towards human civilisation was achieved.

The current interest in the birth of agriculture has not occasioned any slackening of activity to explore the other chapters of Syria's early past. The country – once almost an archaeological no-man's-land – is now host to over thirty foreign archaeological missions, which include Americans, Australians, Belgians, British, Dutch, French, Germans, Italians, Japanese and Poles. Yet it takes a long while for archaeology to present fresh evidence, and for that evidence to be interpreted as history. However, the archaeological discoveries in Syria over the past fifty years have already brought fundamental changes to the way the country's early history and that of the Near East are viewed.

Whilst the successive waves of Semitic migrations from the desert heartland of Arabia into the lands of the Fertile Crescent – firstly the Amorites and Canaanites in the middle of the third millennium BC, and then the Aramaeans and Hebrews towards the end of the second millennium – are still broadly accepted, the presence of an even earlier Semitic population, as revealed in Ebla, raises the possibility that the Eblaites (perhaps along with the Akkadians) were part of an earlier migration. Meanwhile, exploration of the sites of the first agriculturalists points increasingly to a wave of settlement from the north in even remoter times. Whatever fusion of peoples occurred in Syria at the dawn of history, the essential point to emerge from the excavation of Ebla is that Syria was not 'merely a crossroads but rather an original great cultural centre of the ancient world' (Matthiae).

Thus the main achievement of the archaeological exploration of Syria in the twentieth century has been to establish the country as a great field of action in its own right. It is no longer possible to view ancient Syria as a nebulous interspace between the great centres of civilisation such as the Nile Valley, Palestine and Mesopotamia, which were the targets of the pioneers of archaeology in the nineteenth century. Syria's ancient past has re-emerged from the dawn of history with a culture and traditions of its own. It is a process of discovery which will continue for many years to come.

CHAPTER TWO

Aramaeans, Phoenicians, Greeks and Romans

Alexander the Great's defeat of Darius at the battle of Issus in 333 BC is usually taken to mark the beginning of the Greco-Roman period in Syria's history; this era lasted until the founding of Constantinople on the site of ancient Byzantium in AD 330 and the final division of the Roman Empire into its separate eastern and western parts in AD 395. The Roman Conquest, and the incorporation of Syria as a Roman province by Pompey in 64 BC, marks the basic division in terms of historical chronology. Convenient though it is, this broad outline can give the impression that Syria underwent a total cultural transformation at the hands firstly of the Greeks and then of the Romans. But this is far from the truth: if one looks beyond the impressive architectural remains to the roots of popular culture, it is the Aramaeans who maintained the continuity of the Syrian Arab tradition throughout the Greco-Roman period.

The Aramaeans, Semitic nomads who settled in Syria towards the end of the second millennium BC, made a lasting and decisive contribution to Syrian civilisation, and their assimilation and development within the indigenous mould is a potent example of Syria's creative absorption of foreign culture. However, little is known about the physical nature of the Aramaean heritage. Academic opinion has rejected the notion of Aramaean art as a continuation of the imperial Hittite tradition, in spite of the frequent use of Hittite motifs by the Aramaeans. Available archaeological evidence of Aramaean civilisation is restricted to a few sites – notably Tell Halaf and Carchemish, on either side of the Syro-Turkish border – and here it is the architecture and even the building technique which constitute the original contribution of this north Syrian art.

Tell Halaf, in particular, provides the most striking illustration of the originality of the Aramaean architects. On the one hand, they sought to emulate the Assyrians who dominated the region during the ninth to seventh centuries BC. Accordingly, their palaces are decorated with guardian figures such as lions, bulls or monsters carved in relief. The desire of the Aramaeans for the trappings of royalty is documented by the phrase of Kaparu of Guzana (Tell Halaf) in commemoration of the construction of his palace: 'What my fathers did not accomplish I did achieve'. On the other hand, their novel use of the portico was even noted by the Assyrians as a distinctive feature of Aramaean design. It is the same feature identified by Matthiae in the royal palace at Ebla, and which historians of architecture now regard as the direct ancestor of the arrangement of Solomon's Temple. Be that as it may, the palace-sanctuary at Tell Halaf is the most impressive of its type, and although much of the imagery is inspired by Assyrian styles, the bold conception of the portico goes beyond the work of the Mesopotamian sculptors.

The continuing excavations at Ain Dara to the north of Aleppo, following the discovery of the site in 1954, should provide further clues about the Hittite culture which so influenced the Aramaeans. Revealed so far are the richly decorated basalt foundations of a temple-cum-palace where sculpture and architecture are combined to stunningly dramatic effect. The fiercely composed claws of the lion reliefs provide a geometry and structure of considerable strength, while the steps carry design motifs of continuously interlacing circles familiar from later Roman and Byzantine mosaics. The total effect of the ruins at Ain Dara is of a grand, symphonic arrangement. Footprints in the stone paving at the temple entrance suggest an invitation for a deity of great stature to descend from the sky and stand on the sacred spot.

It is worth dwelling on the art and architecture of the Aramaeans, for their work represents a fresh start based mainly on local talent in several regions of Syria. Damascus was the seat of an important Aramaean kingdom during the tenth to eighth centuries BC. It was eventually taken and devastated by the Assyrians under Tiglathpileser III in 732 BC, an event which marked the end of Aram Damascus and the demise of the Aramaeans as a political force in Syria.

But Aramaean culture lived on, thanks to the enterprise and international commerce of its merchants. The Aramaean language adapted the Phoenician alphabet and became the vernacular of the entire region of greater Syria; it thrived even under the Persians, who recognised Aramaic as the official language of their empire which at its zenith extended from India to Ethiopia. It

was the language of the people of Syria throughout the Greco-Roman period –
being best remembered as the language of Jesus Christ and his followers – and
survived as the lingua franca of the Near East until the conquest by the speakers
of Arabic in the seventh century AD*. This linguistic supremacy was entirely due
to the Aramaean merchants who were as successful in overland trade as were the
Phoenicians over the seas.

The Phoenicians were essentially those Canaanites who settled in the coastal
region and henceforth followed a different course to that of their inland cousins.
They emerged as the leading traders of the entire Mediterranean region at about
the beginning of the first millennium BC, and their primacy in the eastern
Mediterranean lasted until 332 BC when Alexander took Tyre. In the west they
survived until 146 BC when the Romans destroyed Carthage. However, Phoenician culture survived well into the Greco-Roman period. In addition to the port
cities of Lebanon, originally known as Tyre, Sidon and Byblos, Phoenicia
consisted of a loose constellation of independent centres which included several
other places along the coast and which extended into present-day Syria. Syria's
Phoenician heritage – in terms of today's international borders – is best
represented by the tiny island of Arwad (or Ruad) which appears to be anchored
off the port of Tartus.

Arwad was one of the Phoenician kingdoms – albeit less powerful than Tyre or
Sidon – whose merchant-sailors held a quasi-monopoly on the main trade routes
of the Mediterranean. They also developed the technique of astral navigation,
sailed round Africa some 2000 years before Vasco da Gama, and spread the use
of the phonetic alphabet (invented by their neighbours in Ugarit) throughout a
network of trading stations in southern Europe and north Africa. Arwad today
shows almost no signs of such an illustrious heritage. The island, a mere 800
metres long and 500 metres at its widest point, is now completely covered by
houses. Having been occupied continuously, the remains of Phoenician Arwad
are limited to some sections of the mighty sea-wall defences which once protected
the island. Yet this kingdom, of rather less than half a square kilometre, was once
powerful enough to found a string of colonies on the Syrian mainland.

These mini-colonies of the Phoenician island kingdom, known as the daugh-
ters of Arwad, are the only survivors of the civilisation that begot them, and
their testimony is both mysterious and obscure. On the outskirts of Tartus, just to
the south of the city, lies the place called Amrit – or to the Greeks, Marathus –

---

*Aramaic is still spoken today in the village of Ma'aloula near Damascus.

which has given rise to considerable archaeological speculation. Among the main monuments are two bizarre 'spindles' (Arabic *maghazil*) standing close to one another, with a third some two hundred metres away. The 'spindles' stand above burial chambers and form part of a larger necropolis. Nearby lies a sanctuary consisting of a sacred pool measuring thirty-eight metres, hewn out of the rock to a depth of three metres, which is fed by a spring from a grotto on the south-east side. The focus of the cult is a five-and-a-half metre high cella located in the middle of the pool. Little is known of the cult itself or of the community which served it. The exact purpose of the sanctuary of the sacred spring, known simply as *al-ma'bid* (temple) is still wrapped in mystery.

Amrit also poses something of an architectural enigma within the context of Syrian building. The style of the sanctuary – with the exception of a temple located at Hosn-Sulayman, seventy kilometres inland from Tartus – is without parallel in Syria and points to a uniquely Phoenician origin in the fifth or fourth century BC. It is postulated that this primitive form of the Phoenician sanctuary was to be developed on a much grander scale and within a different architectural idiom in such majestic buildings as the Temple of Baal in Palmyra and the lost Temple of Jupiter in Damascus. Yet the sanctuary of the spring at Amrit evokes the primeval magic of natural phenomena characteristic of early religions. The sacred pool at Amrit is now overgrown with weeds but still recognisable for what it is, for the spring water can be seen bubbling forth from two small lions' heads; and the view across fields carpeted in spring and summer with wild flowers, to the deep blue of the Mediterranean, is enough to inspire in the onlooker a vague sense of awe and anticipation.

The Phoenician sanctuary at Amrit and the Aramaean palace at Tell Halaf are two striking examples of the old Semitic culture, with beliefs linked to natural forces and the endless cycle of life and death. Though little else remains of the architecture of the millennium prior to the Greco-Roman occupation and although Syria had been invaded and occupied successively by the Assyrians, the Babylonians and the Persians, it should not be imagined that the country had surrendered its ancient identity. The Hellenism which the young, all-conquering Alexander brought into Syria after the battle of Issus certainly breathed new life into the land and stimulated a fresh cultural expression; but the traffic was by no means one-way and Syria still possessed adequate vitality to respond to Hellenism in equal measure.

Syria's Hellenistic experience has left little physical trace. Perishable papyrus replaced clay tablets, providing less epigraphic evidence of the Greek period than exists from the third and second millennia BC. As for Hellenistic architecture in Syria it is represented entirely by buildings constructed in the Roman period on the sites of their Greek predecessors. Only at Dura Europos are there remains of a Hellenistic city. This obliteration of Greek achievements is both unfortunate and ironic, for it was through the medium of the town and its architecture that the successors of Alexander sought to propagate Hellenistic values and ideals.

When the empire of Alexander was shared out, the Seleucid kings, descendants of Seleucus Nicator, one of the Macedonian generals of Alexander's army, claimed most of Syria and established a string of model Greek towns as outposts of Hellenistic culture. Seleucus himself founded a number of towns in Syria, notably Antioch (Antakia)*, Laodicea (present-day al-Ladhiqiya, named after the mother of Seleucus), and Apamea (Afamia, named after his wife). Dura Europos was at this time a military outpost. Other existing cities were renamed and given a Hellenistic gloss.

These cities were a direct expression of Alexander's dream of a brotherhood of man, to which end he had ordered '. . . all men to regard the world as their country . . . good men as their kin, and bad men as foreigners'. Peopled mainly by settlers from Macedonia and retired soldiers from the Seleucid army, the Greek cities in Syria provided the framework for a cultural osmosis between Greek and Oriental concepts. At the most fundamental level many of the Macedonians took local wives. However, the Seleucid cities had the additional function as military communications posts as well as being centres for radiating Hellenistic values. Their general pattern followed the grid system of the typical Greek city with a public square, the *agora*, close to the centre as the focal point for the temples.

The river Orontes (al-A'asi) formed the backbone of Seleucid civilisation in Syria; its chief town was Antioch, which became noted for its architecture, festivities, political forms, amusements and intellectual attainments. Strabo (63 BC – AD 24) described it as 'not much inferior in riches and magnitude to Seleucia-on-the-Tigris and Alexandria in Egypt'. Laodicea was both port and pleasure resort, while Apamea[†] served as the military base. Although all the remains of this city date from the Roman period, Apamea was originally founded by the Seleucids as their main garrison town. The total extent of the

*Antioch (Antakia) is now administered by Turkey.
[†]Since 1983 wide public interest in Syria has been shown in Apamea. Teams of voluntary helpers, notably students and school pioneers, are undertaking the task of re-erecting the columns and the great gate as well as excavating other monuments.

city has not been excavated, since much of the 615-acre site is now farming land, but it is estimated that Apamea in its heyday sheltered a population of some 120,000. It housed the army, the war treasury, and the national stud of 30,000 mares and 300 stallions. Furthermore, it catered for the breeding and training of war elephants, the tanks of antiquity.

Impressive as the statistics are, it must be stressed that overall the Greeks were but a small minority among the overwhelming majority of native Syrians. They sought to rule through the propagation of a superior culture; local deities were tolerated and indeed some were Hellenised. In return, some Greek deities were Syrianised. The benefits of Greek civilisation were generally restricted to the urban middle-classes, with the broad mass of the rural village population probably well outside the orbit of Greek ideas and language. Aramaic continued to be the vernacular – even in the towns – throughout the Greco-Roman period, and Semitic beliefs continued to form the religious outlook of the native Syrian population. At the top end of the social and intellectual scale the Syrians were profoundly influenced by the cultural heritage of Greece, but the urban islands of Hellenism were surrounded by a sea of Semitic custom and failed to create a new national cohesion. The military hold of the Seleucids soon became tenuous as the Parthians from the east, the Armenians from the north and the Nabataeans from the south launched successive invasions which disrupted the trade routes of the hinterland. The century prior to the Roman conquest of Syria was characterised by native revolts, internal dissension, family quarrels and steady loss of territory by the Seleucids. Nevertheless, the Seleucids did lay the foundations of an organised economy and administration that lasted throughout the Roman and Byzantine periods.

The synthetic nature of Greek civilisation in Syria, as well as the shifting political fortunes of the Seleucid rulers, find dramatic illustration in the ruins of Dura Europos, the best preserved of their settlements. Dura was originally founded by Seleucus himself, in about 300 BC, as a relay to serve and protect the trade route along the Euphrates which linked the Gulf with the Mediterranean; but it soon became a frontier town, as the Seleucid realms in Mesopotamia were taken over by the Parthians. Its chequered history on the eastern flank of Syria reflects the troubled international politics of the period, but its importance to archaeologists far exceeds the marginal role it played in the events of its time.

Situated on the west bank of the Euphrates between Deir az-Zor and Abu Kemal, Dura Europos – like its neighbour Mari – was until very recently just another anonymous mound. A British army officer, Capt. M.C. Murphy, was on patrol in the area on 30 March 1920 and reported 'some ancient wall paintings in a wonderful state of preservation'. Within days James Henry Breasted, of the newly established Oriental Institute of the University of Chicago, was sent to investigate. His explorations – due to the political circumstances of the time – were confined to one day, but what he saw was enough: 'It was a startling revelation of the fact that in this deserted stronghold we were standing in a home of ancient Syrian civilisation completely lost to the western world for sixteen centuries'. In fact, as we have seen, Dura's origins go back seven centuries further, to the Seleucid foundation of 300 BC. Breasted's observations were based on the famous mural paintings of the third century AD, in which he immediately detected a link between early Hellenistic-Roman art and that of sixth-century Byzantium, familiar from Ravenna. Breasted's 1922 publication, *The Oriental Forerunners of Byzantine Painting*, focused attention on the much disdained Parthians, who had challenged the might of the Romans. It also brought the site of Dura Europos back into the light of history and led to its subsequent archaeological investigation.

Franz Cumont, the Belgian scholar, was commissioned by the French Academy to dig at Dura in 1922 – 3. The paintings which Breasted had discovered in 1920 had been partially mutilated in the intervening period, but Cumont's two brief digs resulted in the excavation of the 'Temple of the Palmyrene Gods' and the finding of parchments. These confirmed the name of Dura Europos and that Greek and Macedonian settlers had laid out the city. Aerial photos were to provide conclusive evidence that the entire city plan was a grid of streets in the Hippodamean system common to Hellenistic towns. Examination of the walls and some of the principal buildings showed the successive contributions of Greeks, Parthians and Romans. Coins from Phoenicia and Mesopotamia testified to extensive trade links. One of the most spectacular finds was a Roman wooden shield with a leather covering; it bore an illustration of a ship and a list of places between the Black Sea and Syria which had obviously been the itinerary of the soldier whose legion had made the march. Dura thus emerged as the most easterly outpost of the Romans, albeit on a Seleucid site.

The ensuing French-American campaigns, which were carried out between 1928 and 1937, permitted the history of Dura to be reconstructed stage by stage. From its beginning as a fortified caravan city between Antioch and Seleucia-on-the-Tigris to its occupation by the Parthians in around 113 BC, Dura found itself on the sensitive borderline contested by the two superpowers of the time, Rome and Parthia. The peace which Augustus concluded in 20 BC left the city in

Parthian hands. Dura prospered throughout the first century AD and served to facilitate the growing trade across the desert to the oasis city of Palmyra, which was within the Roman orbit. This period of Parthian glory was interrupted by the eastern campaign of Trajan in AD 115 and was finally eclipsed by Verus, who took the city in the name of Rome in AD 164. Dura thus changed from a Parthian town on the Roman border to a Roman outpost on the Parthian flank, sowing the seeds of its subsequent destruction in AD 256 when the Sassanians under Shapur I – the new power in the east – advanced on the Romans, bent on the reconquest of the old Persian Empire.

The circumstances of the final siege and destruction of Dura have been revealed by the archaeologists. The inhabitants evidently anticipated the assault for they took great pains to fortify the walls with vast quantities of rubble and mud-brick against the Sassanians. An incidental result of this activity was the preservation of the frescoes which have been found in excellent condition in buildings close to the walls. However, these measures proved to be futile for the Sassanian sappers succeeded in driving mines under the walls and entering the city. The towers themselves did not collapse entirely, thanks to the embankments which had been set up. The full drama of the final struggle of Dura can be evoked by the skeletons of the soldiers discovered in a collapsed mine. This was the front line of a terrifying underground battle fought out in the stifling darkness. Evidently, the Sassanians either massacred the inhabitants or led them off into captivity, for no more is heard of the city of Dura Europos. In the words of Clark Hopkins, excavator at the site on behalf of Yale University: 'After the siege and victory by the Persians in AD 256 the record is blank. The mute testimony that remained was of a site desolate and forlorn, where the lonely and level sands covered the bones of the city and stretched away across the desert.'

Michael Rostovtzeff, whose account of Dura Europos was published in 1938, likened the site on the Euphrates to that of Pompeii, since the interest of the ruins lay not in their historical importance as the setting for great events but in their beautiful state of preservation. The discovery of so many perishable items – from the frescoes themselves to objects of wood, leather, textile and paper – allows insights into the daily life of the city. But above all it is the works of art discovered in Dura Europos which have done most to stimulate academic discussion and which have provided the basis for new theories about the precise interaction of the Greek, Parthian and Roman cultures.

Rostovtzeff postulated that the artistic evidence of Dura Europos – now to be found in the National Museum in Damascus and the Art Gallery of Yale

University – shows that Hellenism in the Orient was 'no more than a veneer'. Certainly, the Macedonians allowed the local gods to be honoured in temples of oriental plan, but it should not be considered surprising to find such a strong Parthian influence in a place which was occupied by that people for over two hundred years. Perhaps more to the point is the novel way in which Parthian and Hellenistic art mixed and developed in Dura Europos. The archaeological and artistic evidence of Dura Europos is not conclusive enough to permit new theories of cultural osmosis, but it does illustrate most vividly a chapter in Syria's history when Greco-Roman and Parthian values interacted, though they were in opposition. Throughout all the international struggles, the basic population of Dura – and of Syria as a whole – remained thoroughly Semitic. But dramatic though it was, the protracted battle for Dura Europos was no more than a sideshow in the unfolding epic of the Roman occupation of Syria.

The mainstream of the Roman era in Syria, so confidently inaugurated by Pompey in 64 BC, proceeded to evolve on a majestic scale in the Greek cities previously founded by the Seleucids. An unsteady beginning, under the pro-consuls Gabinius, Crassus, Cassius and Mark Antony was transformed, with the elevation of Octavian in 27 BC as Augustus, into Syria's golden age under the Pax Romana. Peace and stability now created the framework for the prosperity of Syria. The Romans – unlike their Seleucid predecessors – concentrated on military control and sound administration rather than cultural expansion. Theirs was a practical outlook: Syria was a frontier state against the Parthians but at the same time it was a source of taxes and a land with great agricultural potential. Under Roman auspices an amazing diversity of semi-autonomous local communities were permitted to exist, ranging from the Greek-type cities to priest-kings and tribal chiefs. In Damascus, the Nabataeans maintained their authority in return for a lump sum in tribute.

New irrigation schemes in the Orontes valley and the Hauran – including areas which are now treeless – made Syria one of the most productive agricultural countries in the Roman Empire, famed for its superfluity of grain, wine and oil. But it was in the architectural domain that the Roman achievement was the most decisive and enduring. There was a boom in both urban and rural building projects. Syrian city life in the first century BC was described by Posidonius, native of Apamea (135 – 51 BC): 'There were many clubs in which they amused themselves continuously, using the gymnasia as baths, anointing themselves with expensive oil and unguents, and using the schools, for so they called the dining-halls of their members, as if they were their own houses, stuffing themselves there for the greater part of the day with wines and food, and even carrying off much besides, amidst the sound of noisy lyres, which made whole cities ring with the uproar.'

Doubtless the Romans, who by this time had assimilated Greek culture, found themselves immediately at home in the Seleucid cities of Syria, and the combination of Greek and Roman concepts in Syria was to prove highly successful. The Romans provided the political, military and administrative strength which the Greeks lacked, but in turn learned from the Greeks in matters of art and philosophy. Greek was to remain the language of culture and Aramaic the vernacular but Latin was used for administrative purposes. Thus Hellenism contrived to live on in Syria under the protection of the Romans.

The native Syrians – a population which by this time included descendants of Alexander's Macedonian armies alongside the descendants of the Amorites, Canaanites and Aramaeans – responded to the opportunities which the Roman Empire provided. In commerce, Syrian merchants proved to be far sharper even than their Roman counterparts; they travelled throughout the lands ruled by Rome and at the same time kept a tight monopoly on the rich trade that passed through Syria itself. Myrrh and incense from South Arabia, spices and jewels from India, silk from China were all channelled through the trade counters of the Syrian merchants. Syrian influence also made itself felt back in Rome, and Juvenal's famous lament was aimed at more than just Syrian entertainers: 'The Syrian Orontes has long since poured its water into the Tiber, bringing with it its lingo and its manners, its flutes and its slanting harp string.' As the years passed, Syrian ambitions, even to the imperial purple, became reality.

This process began with the marriage of Julia Domna, a daughter of Emesa (Homs), to Septimius Severus in AD 187, and continued with his subsequent reign as Emperor from AD 193 to 211. After his death, Julia Domna held on to power through her son Caracalla, who in AD 212 decreed that Roman citizenship be bestowed on all free residents of the provinces, thus making all Syrians into Romans and giving them all the privileges of that status. Following the murder of Caracalla and the suicide of Julia Domna, Syrian interests in Rome continued to be promoted by Julia Maesa, her more capable sister, who conspired to have her grandson Elagabulus enthroned. Semitic belief during the reign of Elagabulus was promoted to such a great extent that the worship of the Syrian deity Emesene Baal became supreme in the Roman world. The rule of Elagabulus, however, sank into debauchery and acts of extravagant folly, though the family record was redeemed by another grandson of Julia Maesa,

Alexander Severus, who ruled the Roman Empire from AD 222 to 235.

Perhaps the most remarkable of the Syrian emperors was Philip the Arab – hailed in AD 244 by the Syrian army as Emperor, a decision soon ratified by the Senate. Philip's meteoric rise to imperial power was probably a reflection of the growing importance of Syria as a military power, but his five years as Emperor are remembered more for the elevation of his native village to a mini-metropolis than for any act of international significance: the hamlet of Shahba in the Hauran became the city of Philippopolis.

The Hauran plateau had been under the control of the Nabataeans in Petra during the early years of the Roman presence in Syria. However, in AD 106, the Nabataeans' independent rule came to an end and in its place the Roman Province of Arabia was installed with its capital at Bosra. The physical benefits of Roman civilisation were promptly and lavishly bestowed on the region through a vast programme of public works. The Roman achievement in the Hauran can still be appreciated today; although surrounded by the clutter of country life the fine buildings have not been entirely obliterated and the splendours of the past can easily be reconstructed in the imagination.

Bosra, befitting its status as provincial capital, 'Nova Trajana Bostra', soon acquired the Roman trappings of triumphal arches, colonnaded markets, sumptuous baths and an imposing theatre. The theatre of Bosra – still miraculously intact inside a mediaeval Arab fortification – is now the main reason for the fame of the city, as the venue for an annual cultural festival. Yet the real achievement of the Romans in Bosra – and indeed in the Hauran in general – should not be sought in individual buildings but in the immense outpouring of wealth and energy into the maximum development of somewhat meagre resources. The true story of the Hauran in Roman times must begin with the irrigation works and agricultural exploitation of a region whose potential was continually hampered by drought, locusts and marauding bedouin tribes.

The same determination which created the farming boom of the Hauran was also applied to the craft of stone masonry. The work of the local sculptors shows a vitality of its own which overcame the rather thankless task of transforming black basaltic rock into elegant and pleasing forms. The Hauran achieved renown for its vigorous and bountiful production of stone images. It is not the fault of the craftsmen if the sombre tone of the material employed both in building and sculpture contrives to create an overall effect of melancholy; for after the dazzling spectacle of marble and the warm impression of limestone, the ubiquitous black basalt of the Hauran lies heavy on the eye. The beautiful mosaics –

which have come through the ages so well preserved and are now housed in Philippopolis and Suweida – give a clear indication of the refinement and sophisticated lifestyle in the Hauran during the second to fourth centuries AD under the Pax Romana.

As the physical and artistic development of the Hauran proceeded apace, so the region became linked to the Roman communications network in Syria, which extended north to Antioch and east to Dura Europos and the Euphrates borderlands. The Roman roads were the basic prior condition to prosperity, while security and efficient transport were the essential factors in promoting trade. Much of the Roman road system in Syria has been lost or obliterated in later times but there is near Aleppo a famous stretch of the Chalcis–Antioch road whose huge stone slabs more than a foot thick give a vivid impression of the sheer weight and volume of Rome's achievement in Syria. Elsewhere the roads can be detected from the air, as was so dramatically revealed by Père Poidebard, a pioneer of aerial archaeology; his survey of Syria in the years 1925 – 32 is still an essential reference.

Roman road-building served basically a military purpose. Throughout their stay in Syria the Romans were confronted by hostile neighbours to the east, first the Parthians and then the Sassanians, and the road system reflects the defensive preoccupations of the time. The outer limit of communications was backed by an inner ring of roads which would permit traffic to continue even if the enemy managed to control the peripheral roads. Thus the concept of the border known as the *limes* came to encompass not just the frontier line itself but an entire zone on the eastern flank of the Roman Empire. The system is largely to the credit of the Emperor Diocletian, whose name was conferred on the main artery of the Roman road network in Syria, the Strata Diocletiana.

The opening up of the Syrian desert was greatly facilitated by the road engineers of Rome. Wells were sunk at precise intervals of twenty-four miles to serve the needs of the vast camel-caravans which took the short cut across the desert from the Euphrates to the cities of Emesa (Homs), Damascus and the Syrian coast. Availability of water was the overriding factor in the development of the caravan routes. Thus it was that a small oasis with a generous spring of drinkable, though sulphurous, water found itself at a strategic point in the heart of the Syrian desert, where the roads of a booming international commerce were suddenly to converge. By the end of the first century AD the tiny village of Tadmor was firmly launched on a brilliant if short-lived career as one of the most flamboyant and spectacular civilisations of its day; wealthy beyond all expectation, with enough power and self-confidence to challenge even the might of imperial Rome. The rise and fall of Palmyra, as Tadmor came to be known, occupied only 300 years, a mere grain of sand in the hour-glass of Syrian history, but the spectacular ruins of the city known as the 'Bride of the Desert' have kept alive the memory of its prosperous merchant community.

Palmyra had begun to prosper during the first century BC, prior to the arrival of the Romans in Syria, and by 41 BC was already important enough to attract the attention of Mark Antony, who launched an abortive raid against the oasis town. The Palmyrenes received intelligence of the Roman approach and withdrew to the safety of the Euphrates, carrying with them their property. This can be seen as a significant indication that Palmyra at the time was still basically a nomadic settlement and that its valuables could be removed at short notice on camel-back. A century later, Palmyra had acquired such wealth that a sudden evacuation would have been out of the question. The flight to the Euphrates – the Parthians were then in control of the region and had occupied the Seleucid fortress town of Dura Europos – can also be taken as a sign of Palmyra's eastward-looking attitude. Indeed, it was the vital link between Palmyra and Dura Europos which permitted the rich commerce between East and West, in spite of the mutual hostility of Romans and Parthians.

Throughout the first century AD, Palmyra grew steadily in prosperity as a buffer-state and trade emporium between Rome and Parthia, maintaining a semi-independent status but receiving substantial financial and technical help from Rome. The Temple of Baal followed Roman techniques but the layout of the sanctuary was adapted to traditional Semitic lines. The Palmyrenes soon mastered and moulded to their own taste the architectural and artistic lessons of Rome and went on to develop their own distinctive style.

After AD 106 the eclipse of Petra, that other caravan city which received the rich commerce of South Arabia, worked to the immense advantage of Palmyra. Money poured into the city, both in the form of trading profits and of taxes levied on goods in transit and on the supply of water. The so-called 'tariff' of Palmyra, now in the Hermitage Museum in Leningrad, gives details of the meticulous financial administration of Palmyra, whose merchants expressed their wealth in grandiose, urban schemes. A monumental arch guides the street from the Temple of Baal around a 30° bend, before debouching into the main thoroughfare of colonnades, one of the most magnificent streets to have survived from the Greco-Roman period. Even today in its ruined state this great urban highway speaks of the prosperity and ambition of the citizens of Palmyra.

Trade and profit were the true gods of the city; successful merchants were honoured by statues mounted prominently on the columns of the main colonnade street, and the throng of Palmyrenes must have been impressed as they looked up to the seemingly endless line of stone and bronze effigies of their ancestors. Vast caravans of up to two to three thousand camels plied between Palmyra and Dura Europos and on to Seleucia-on-the-Tigris to meet others from Persia, India and China, with their loads of silk, jade, ebony, spices, ivory, pearls and precious stones. The small remnants of Chinese silk discovered in a tomb in Palmyra and now displayed in the National Museum in Damascus are a potent evocation of the luxury trade of the first century AD.

Palmyra's fortunes continued to rise throughout the second century AD and reached their zenith in the third-century rule of Odenath, whose services to the Romans against the Sassanians were rewarded with the title 'Corrector of the East'. His wife, Zenobia, who probably had a hand in his assassination, set her sights on even greater things. Styling herself 'Queen of the East', and her son Vaballath 'King of Kings', Zenobia's ambitions were as imperialist as those of Rome itself. Having declared Palmyrene independence, Zenobia defeated a Roman force, invaded Asia Minor and Egypt – and for a brief period around AD 267 – 72, loomed large as the rising power in the east. But Palmyra, for all its wealth, was no match for Rome. Zenobia was captured by Aurelian's troops on the banks of the Euphrates as she attempted to escape to the Sassanian side. Legend has it that she was led into Rome in chains of gold as the jewel in Aurelian's triumph, but the fate that befell her proud city was a more violent humiliation. At first, after the defeat and capture of Zenobia, Aurelian had spared Palmyra, but when his garrison was massacred by the people of Palmyra, he returned to ravage the city.

Although there was to be some recovery in the Byzantine period, this punitive campaign effectively marked the end of Palmyra's greatness. The city suffered repeatedly at the hands of bedouin raiders and gradually it was reclaimed by the desert. According to later Islamic tradition, Palmyra was the work of Solomon, who bade the *jinns* construct the fine buildings through their magic – for how else could such a magnificent city have been built in such a spot?

As for Zenobia, she ended her days in exile in a comfortable villa by the Tiber. Gibbon's description of this flamboyant desert queen is a flattering epitaph: 'She . . . equalled in beauty her ancestor Cleopatra, and far surpassed that princess in chastity and valour. Zenobia was esteemed the most lovely as well as the most heroic of her sex. She was of dark complexion . . . Her teeth were of a pearly whiteness, and her large, black eyes sparkled with uncommon fire, tempered by the most attractive sweetness. Her voice was strong and harmonious. Her manly understanding was strengthened and adorned by study.' This is the portrait of a true heroine, and it is no wonder that Zenobia is remembered as the flower of Arabian womanhood. On the other hand her military achievement must be stressed: this was a woman who would march on foot for miles at the head of her troops. Finally, we must not forget her supreme act of folly in challenging Rome, for the ruins of Palmyra are her personal legacy.

For centuries, Palmyra's scattered columns lay forgotten by the world at large, awaiting eventual rediscovery. First reports of the abandoned city were relayed to Europe by the Italian traveller, Pietro della Valle, in 1616 and 1625, then by the Frenchman, Jean-Baptiste Tavernier, in 1630; but it was a group of English merchants living in Aleppo who organised in 1678 and 1691 the first proper expeditions.

Dr Huntington's 1678 expedition ended in a fiasco, as the band of English merchants were ambushed and robbed – even of their clothes – by the desert nomads or 'mountain Arabs', as they were described by their victims. In 1691 a second expedition was mounted from Aleppo; this time the journey was success-fully accomplished and the account published by the clergyman Dr William Halifax, *Relation of a Voyage to Tadmor* (1695), gives some fascinating insights into conditions in Palmyra at the end of the seventeenth century. Most strikingly, the settlement was by then so reduced that it consisted of only some thirty to forty families living in 'little huts made of dirt within ye walls of a spacious court, which enclosed a most magnificent heathen temple'. In other words, the Temple of Baal now sheltered the entire Palmyrene population, a fact which caused Dr Halifax to wonder at 'ye greatest state and magnificence together with ye extremity of filth and poverty'. Like others who were to follow, Dr Halifax gave full and spontaneous expression to the awe-inspiring sight of the ruins and his words may serve as a typical reaction of travellers arriving at Palmyra: 'You have ye prospect of such magnificent ruines, yet if it be lawful to frame a conjecture of ye original beauty of ye place by what is still remaining I question whether any city in ye world could have challenged the precedence of this in its glory.'

Words alone cannot do justice to the glory of Palmyra, for it is above all a visual experience which needs to be seen to be believed. Fortunately, as early as 1751, Palmyra was visited by two engravers and illustrators of singular talent, Wood and Dawkins, whose book *The Ruins of Palmyra* appeared in 1753. This beautiful edition coincided with the fashion for neoclassical design and architecture in England and instantly became a source of inspiration for builders and decorators. As a result, many an English country house has incorporated some features of Palmyra which may be traced back to the engravings of Wood and Dawkins. Other notable visitors who braved the rigours and perils of the trip to Palmyra included Volney (1787), L-F. Cassas (1790s), Marquis de Vogüé (1853) and Waddington (1861). Yet the most memorable of all was surely the aristocratic Lady Hester Stanhope, whose colourful exploits in the Levant attained their summit in the ruins of Zenobia's city.

Lady Hester left England in 1810 with a small group of companions on an extensive journey through the lands of the Eastern Mediterranean. Her reception by the Pasha in Damascus greatly appealed to her regal instincts and the idea of the trip to Palmyra was doubtless inspired by the legend of the famous Arabian queen. According to Dr Meryon, whose *Travels of Lady Hester Stanhope* appeared in 1846: 'She sought the remains of Zenobia's greatness, as well as the ruins of Palmyra.' Whatever her true motivation, her behaviour and comportment were in the tradition of a royal progress: 'I carried everything before me, and was crowned under the triumphal arch . . .' The aura of Zenobia's greatness in Palmyra is still enough to fill the ruins and stir imaginations less romantic than that of Lady Hester Stanhope.

Proper archaeological exploration and excavation of Palmyra did not commence until the beginning of this century. The German Archaeological Mission worked on the site from 1902 to 1917 and provided the groundwork for the subsequent digs. Today's visitor cannot immediately be aware of how much physical toil has been expended simply on the clearance of the site; an aerial photograph taken in the 1920s shows the mud-brick houses of Tadmor still huddled within the walls of the enclosure surrounding the Temple of Baal, but in 1929 the new township of Tadmor was created and the entire population removed to some distance from the ruins. Some monuments such as the Tetrapylon – that imposing group of columns which provides a visual counterpoint to the monumental arch – have been reconstructed by the Department of Antiquities. Other buildings have been partially restored, but the work of routine and necessary maintenance of the ruins is in itself a major undertaking. The illustrations from the eighteenth and nineteenth centuries show all too clearly how much has been lost during the past two hundred years. The preservation and presentation of ancient Palmyra is an endless task, quite separate from the further archaeological investigation of the site.

Excavations have also revealed the agricultural potential of the oasis. The spring itself supplies about 150 litres per second of sulphurous water from a grotto over 100 metres in length*; and about to kilometres to the north-west there is another sweet spring, showing evidence of Stone Age and Bronze Age occupation. Remains of a dam and an irrigation system indicate that the Palmyrenes managed to cultivate the desert fringe and produce adequate supplies of cereals which were supplemented by the import of other foods from east and west. The notion of a city in the desert is thus a simplification, for Palmyra – under proper management of its natural resources – was able to support a sizeable population.

As for the people of Palmyra, their images – albeit in idealised form – have been preserved not in the statues they erected to themselves in the Colonnade Street but in the funerary monuments which they had carved as a ritual expression of their passage into eternity. These statues have been discovered in Palmyra's 'City of the Dead', ironically in a better state of preservation than those in the 'City of the Living'. The tombs are housed in three types of structure: hypogea (or crypts), small house-type mausolea, and tower tombs. The latter, of which the largest are five storeys high, are the most distinctively Palmyrene in style. Equally distinctive are the sculptures of Palmyra. Greco-Roman technique is much in evidence, but the treatment, especially that famous frontality, sets them apart from any classical models. We see entire families in flowing robes, arranged in groups, apparently calm in the expectation that their life beyond the grave would continue at the same social level as that which they had previously maintained. There are also individual busts, clearly recognisable as human personalities, yet at the same time curiously metamorphosed into the ideal types which they would assume in the afterlife. Preoccupation with death and the world beyond underlies the entire spectrum of Palmyrene statuary that we have before us today. It is probably a one-sided view of a civilisation which enjoyed to such an extent the pleasures and riches of this life.

By the time of Palmyra's destruction by Aurelian in AD 272 the Roman Empire was already being transformed from within. Throughout the lands ruled by Rome, Christianity was in the ascendant. This was nowhere more obvious than in Syria, where all the Greco-Roman sites were soon to become major centres of the Christian faith. But Roman rule in Syria was not brought to an end – as it was in Europe – by internal revolt, cultural fatigue, or the challenge of a

---

*The spring can still be visited just opposite the Meridien Hotel in Palmyra.

new invader. On the contrary, Rome renewed its energy and inspiration from within, removed to Constantinople and donned a Greek-Christian mantle. In Syria it continued to thrive for another three hundred years, until the conquests of the Muslim Arabs in the seventh century.

In many ways, the cultural legacy of the Romans was limited; Latin never took hold and Aramaic thrived as the vernacular not only of Syria but of the Near East as a whole. On the other hand, Roman expertise and administration created the framework of peace and prosperity which was the prior condition to the flowering of Syrian civilisation. It is therefore fitting that architecture, that most practical of the arts, remains as the most lasting monument to the Roman presence in Syria.

CHAPTER THREE

The Cradle
of Christianity

Christians nowadays tend to overlook the Syrian chapter in their religious and cultural heritage. The concept of the 'Holy Land' is rather narrowly defined as Palestine, encompassing Jerusalem, Bethlehem and Nazareth. Yet Syria not only witnessed the birth and immediate impact of the new faith, but in the early centuries also produced the most fervent response to its message in both a spiritual and a material sense.

The presence of Syria's first Christian converts is attested by the account in the *Acts of the Apostles* of the conversion of Saul of Tarsus, scourge of the followers of Christ. Saul was, of course, on his way to Damascus in the pursuit of his bloody persecutions – which had included his 'consenting unto' the stoning of Stephen – and was intent upon the rooting out of the Christian community in that city when he was blinded by divine light. Meanwhile, his redemption was being prepared through the person of Ananias (Hanania), a Christian resident of Damascus, who received a vision instructing him to 'go into the street which is called Straight, and inquire in the house of Judas for one called Saul of Tarsus. . .' The street which is called 'Straight' is still the dominant feature of the plan of the old city and it owes its existence to the original *via recta* of the Roman period. From the east gate known as Bab Sharqi it extends for about a mile to the bazaar known as the Suq al-Tawil, or the long bazaar. There is now a small mosque built on what is thought to be the site of the house of Judas, but the memory of the house of Ananias is better preserved. Immediately to the right, after entering the Bab Sharqi, a road leads directly to the underground chapel of Saint Ananias, within the remains of what was once a large Byzantine church built on the spot occupied by the house of Ananias. The tiny chapel is lit by an opening in the vault, through which the dazzling sunshine sometimes penetrates the subterranean gloom with such an intense shaft of light as to be almost tangible. A series of painted panels on the walls narrate the life and travels of St Paul – as Saul of Tarsus came to be known – which included most of the lands of the eastern Mediterranean, and finally Rome itself where Paul eventually found martyrdom by the sword.

Paul's stay in Damascus is of interest for the light it sheds on the strength and organisation of the very first Christian communities in Syria. His subsequent career underlines the pre-eminence of Antioch, which continued to eclipse Damascus in the early centuries of the Christian era, just as it had since its founding by the Seleucids. It was from this city that the newly converted Paul embarked on several of his missionary journeys, and it was also to Antioch that he returned to give account of his proselytising. The first circle of disciples of Christ to call themselves Christians was based at Antioch; so, in a sense, the designation 'Christian' may be traced back to the mother of churches in that city which can be regarded as the original headquarters of organised Christianity. This role was greatly enhanced after the destruction of Jerusalem by the Romans under Titus in AD 70, which left Antioch as the sole capital of Christendom.

Gradually the Christian faith penetrated the fabric of the Roman Empire and, despite its outlaw status and the frequent persecution of its followers, it contrived to bring about the most spectacular non-violent revolution from within. In AD 306 Constantine became co-Emperor, and having undergone in 312 a conversion to Christianity as dramatic as that of Saul of Tarsus, accorded by the Edict of Milan in 313 complete toleration of Christianity throughout the Empire. The 'Peace of the Church' inaugurated by the Edict of Milan was, however, more than an amnesty for persecuted Christians; it heralded the triumph of Christianity over paganism. This conversion of an empire was given even more substance with the founding of Constantinople in 330 on the site of ancient Byzantium. This eastward shift of the Roman Empire worked to the great advantage of the Province of Syria, which was poised for a most spectacular physical and religious expansion. Following the final split of the Roman Empire into its eastern and western halves in 395, the age of Byzantium and of Christianity's brief but glorious reign in Syria was set to unfold.

Seen from a Western perspective, the years following the transfer of power to Constantinople are characterised by the decline and fall of the Roman Empire;

the underlying trend in Europe was of military, administrative and economic collapse. The situation in the east was by contrast one of prosperity and expansion. The fourth to seventh centuries in Syria in particular saw a happy coincidence of commercial and agricultural growth coupled with the unfolding energy of the Christian faith. Antioch soon rivalled the glories of Constantinople and Alexandria. It was as if three hundred years of pent-up religious emotion were suddenly released and given expression in monuments of stone. Churches, hospices, monasteries, shrines and basilicas as well as countless houses and other secular buildings proliferated in all parts of the country. In this spontaneous outburst of Syrian energies Byzantium did not impose its own style. Instead Syrian builders and architects appear to have re-interpreted earlier Hellenistic models and infused them with their own vigorous and original thought and creativity. Nor was their style a uniform response, for the differing physical and geographical conditions led to strongly individual regional characteristics.

In the Hauran in the south, the black basalt was the exclusive material for walls, arches and domes; its brittleness made it difficult to work, with the result that carvings are scarcely in evidence and tend to be flat. In the desert region of the north-east there is a strange combination of basalt and brick, both of the baked and sun-dried varieties; this is best seen in the ruins of the church known as Qasr Ibn Wardan which – exceptionally for this period in Syrian architecture – is directly inspired by Byzantine models. Along the Euphrates and the desert fringes, the frontier towns of Resafa and Halabiya glint mysteriously through the white and grey gypsum of their respective fortifications. However, it is above all in the limestone region of north Syria that Christian architecture found its most articulate expression. Fortunately, the so called 'Dead Cities' of the region between Aleppo, Antioch and Apamea have left behind such extensive and well preserved ruins as to permit an accurate assessment of the height of early Christian civilisation.

It has been suggested that the 'Dead Cities' should actually be called villages, for these 700 settlements contain an average of twenty to fifty houses, although some, like al-Bara (0.5 by 2 kilometres), were the size of towns. Furthermore, there is a lack of urban layout: the houses are grouped together loosely without paved roads or squares and maximum space is devoted to cultivation of food produce. Significantly, there are no signs of any fortification, demonstrating their origin in an era of peace and stability. On the other hand, their designation as 'cities' is deserved on account of the solidity and elegance of the houses which would do justice to any urban centre. Fortunately, many of the houses are in an excellent state of preservation, missing only their roofs and floors; it is as if their occupants walked out at some time in the eighth century and no one has been there since. Apart from a few scattered farming communities making provisional use of the remaining structures, mostly as enclosures for sheep and goats, what was once a heavily populated region is today almost completely deserted. The 'Dead Cities' are ghost towns in the real sense of the term.

In the fifth to seventh centuries the inhabitants of these comfortable houses would have looked out onto a very different landscape from that of today. Now the soil has been eroded, revealing the gnarled limestone substratum, the skeleton of what was once a gentle, living countryside of carefully tended vineyards and olive groves. The hundreds of oil and wine-presses indicate that Syrian produce was much in demand. It has also been put forward that the leisured classes of Antioch would have repaired to this bucolic environment in order to recharge their batteries, much in the manner of weekend tourism from the large cities of the present day. However, the houses point rather to a hard-working society of independent farmers with no evidence either of rich land-owners or of serfs, although neither can be ruled out entirely.

Yet the 'Dead Cities' are more than simply a high-water mark of human settlement, for the underlying inspiration of these prosperous communities was nascent Syrian Christianity. This is clearly demonstrated in the quantity and quality of the religious architecture; indeed, it is the churches of the 'Dead Cities' which have earned the praise of architectural historians as the flower of north Syrian style, towering far above all else at the time. Howard C. Butler noted in his *Early Churches in Syria*: 'There was no era in the architectural history of the western world between the Roman period of the second century and the revival of the building art in northern Europe during the twelfth, that produced monuments of stone architecture comparable to those of Syria between the fourth and the seventh centuries.' Butler's observations were made during the Princeton University Archaeological Expeditions to Syria in 1904–5 and 1909 and what he revealed to the academic world was largely new material. But he had been preceded by Count Melchior de Vogüé, whose two formidable tomes, *Syrie Centrale. Architecture civile et religieuse du Ier au VIIIe siècle* (1865–77), described eighteen churches, of which twelve are in the north. More recent works by J. Mattern (1933–44), J. Lassus (1947) and G. Tchalenko (1953–8) have added considerably to our knowledge of the 'Dead Cities' and further emphasised the unique cultural achievement already so unequivocally commended by Butler.

Happily for the layman, the architectural impact is such that recourse to learned books is unnecessary for an appreciation of the freshness, vitality and artistry of the churches. From the smallest chapel such as Deirouni to the magnificent basilicas of Qalb Lozeh and Qala'at Sama'an, the work of the architects and stonemasons is like a revival of the Hellenistic spirit, but with an entirely new dimension of design added by the Syrian craftsmen. It is hardly necessary when contemplating these churches to make any distinction between architect, builder and carver, for the design motifs appear to spring out of the very nature of the stone and to determine the structure as well. Most distinctive are the mouldings around doors and windows which develop such self-confidence that eventually they form a continuous sweep of movement totally encompassing the building.

But if the overall effect is the perfect combination of proportion and decoration, then closer inspection reveals that the stones are of all sizes, simply smoothed, and assembled as they were extracted from the quarry. Yet their various shapes and masses are totally submerged in the overall form of the building. The limestone blocks were fitted together perfectly without any use of mortar, and the exposed surface of stone was then carved to create a design which overruled the construction details. This completely original Syrian idea owed nothing to Byzantium, which, by contrast, tended to hide the walls and columns behind a rich veneer of marble and mosaics mounted on a thick layer of mortar. The Syrian technique has justified itself over the years for today we can appreciate the bare ruins as works of intrinsic beauty, whereas no Byzantine structure is wholly convincing deprived of its ornamental covering. The 'Dead Cities' of north Syria thus represent one of the last flourishes of modest, uncomplicated notions of design achieved through simple means before more ecstatic visions of Christian architecture took over in the Middle Ages. It is mooted, however, that Syrian craftsmen and architects, whose work was interrupted in full spate by the Muslim Arab conquests of the seventh century, moved on partly to Europe, where some centuries later they helped the Romanesque style achieve its definitive shape.

The most famous of all the early churches built in Syria is undoubtedly the majestic edifice dedicated to St Simeon. This is one of the most monumental religious buildings of the first thousand years of the Christian era and it stands, both in its architecture and its engineering, as the sublime expression of the fervour aroused by the new faith. As a building it speaks for itself, but to appreciate how it came into being it is necessary to examine the life of the saint whose memory is enshrined within and to understand the spiritual mood of the time.

Following the Edict of Milan in 313 Christianity was legalised, but by the same token it was to lose the mainspring of its heroism which had been symbolised by the courage and faith of the martyrs. With the threat of martyrdom removed, and then with positive encouragement to convert to Christianity as the official religion of the Eastern Roman Empire, vast numbers of people became Christians and countless others came out into the open to worship God in the name of the new religion. What was gained in numbers was inevitably lost in intensity. The ardent believers who in earlier times would have been proud to be martyred in the name of Christ looked with some feeling of disdain and frustration on the spectacle of Christianity professed by so many people of dubious religious conviction. It was thus as a reaction to the popularisation of the faith that the ascetic movement was born. The spirit of the martyrs lived on in the ascetics or mortifiers of the flesh of the new age, or the 'martyrs of peace' as they have come to be known. These men of profound religious emotion sought through an ingenious variety of acts of self-torture to overcome sufficiently their physical being as to become like angels. This asceticism made a deep impression on the common people, who understood instinctively the motivation behind what, in terms of today's awareness, are often portrayed as acts of lunacy and fanaticism. There can be no mistaking the popular, and indeed, official veneration for the self-inflicted sufferings of the 'martyrs of peace'. St Simeon's life helped set the pattern for many who were to follow.

What we know of Simeon is mainly from the account of his contemporary, Theodoret, Bishop of Cyr. Simeon was born in 390 and was soon drawn to the monastic life, where his aptitude for asceticism brought him both the admiration and jealousy of his brother monks. Removing from the little monastery at Telanissos he took up a semi-hermitic existence on a nearby hill, where he further circumscribed his existence by attaching himself to a large rock on a chain ten metres in length. Even at this early stage in his career, before he adopted the stylitism for which he is chiefly remembered, Simeon was an object of popular veneration and curiosity and the goal of frequent pilgrimages. Theodoret refers to 'a human river' of pilgrims coming from as far away as Armenia, Persia, Spain, Greece, Italy, Gaul and Britain. Icons of Simeon were, it seems, popular in Rome as a token of security.

However, the constant pressure of crowds of people, all anxious to touch Simeon as a talisman, inspired his genial idea of mounting on a column. This was no doubt suggested by the availability of much Greco-Roman masonry lying about. It proved to be the perfect solution: Simeon passed out of reach of the multitude and at the same time remained within the midst of the people come to admire him. His first column was a modest ten feet but as the idea took on he progressed to columns of twenty, thirty-seven and finally sixty feet, which must have been the maximum possible for his voice to be heard by those gathered below. Thus, he remained a stylite from 422 until his death in 459, living suspended 'between heaven and earth', 'like an angel in mortal flesh' and shining 'like the light of the candle' (Theodoret) for all to see. The stylite movement was born.

There is little left of the column of St Simeon, around which the great church was later to be built, but recent research done on the sites occupied by other stylite monks in Syria and published by the Studium Biblicum Franciscanum under the title *Les Stylites Syriens* (1975), allows a partial reconstruction of how life atop such a column was organised. The columns varied between two-and-a-half and six feet in diameter and were provided with a platform and a waist-high railing for security. Some stylites had a small hut or tent to protect themselves against the elements whereas others, such as Simeon, had no protection except the hooded monk's habit. On a fine spring day with a gentle breeze to temper the heat of the sun, it is possible for a moment to put oneself in the situation of a stylite and enjoy the commanding view over the pleasant countryside. However, the climate of north Syria swings from the extreme heat of summer to icy blasts of wind and snow from the Taurus in winter, so that for most of the year extreme physical discomfort would be experienced. Those who sought to emulate the example of Simeon required a robust constitution. There are cases reported of a stylite who lost his monk's habit in a high wind and almost froze to death, and of another who had to be rescued unconscious from under a layer of snow and coaxed back to life by the application of sponges soaked in hot water.

Health and hygiene must also be considered. Illnesses were accepted as an act of God, and the little medical treatment that was available was generally refused. Simeon himself is reported to have had a septic wound in his leg which was so putrescent that an unbelievable number of worms fell from it, and as a result he stood for a whole year on one foot only. Yet in spite of the rigours of the life, stylite monks frequently lived to an advanced age. Simeon himself was sixty-nine when he died, after thirty-seven years on his column; Daniel was aloft for thirty-three years before he died at the age of eighty-four, Alypius reached ninety-nine, Luke 100 and Mar Michel 105 years of age.

Dieticians might ascribe such longevity to the simple vegetarian regime which was probably only slightly different from that of a mountain peasant of the day.

Possibly the daily prostrations in prayer were also an aid to bodily fitness. One observer counted Simeon perform 1244 prostrations before losing count. Throughout the day the stylite would be standing and frequently delivering speeches or sermons to the crowd below. It is documented that Simeon took an active part in the religious controversies of his time and often passed gratuitous pieces of advice to the ecclesiastical authorities in Antioch and Constantinople. It has been suggested that the preaching stylite could be the prototype of the Muslim muezzin, giving the call to prayer from the top of a minaret.

Close study of the stylite way of life has revealed the strategic positioning of the columns close to the established highways of the time; indeed, Simeon chose a spot overlooking the road from Apamea to Cyrrhus. It must have been common for travellers at that time to notice the silhouettes of these columns and be drawn to them to hear the message of those men of God, who lived between heaven and earth. Thus, in their physical elevation the stylite monks were not removed from this world but took an active part in the spreading of the faith in the world below.

The success of their apostolic activity cannot be doubted. The phenomenon of stylitism had a profound influence on the religious awareness of the highest in the land as well as the broad mass of humanity. Such was the belief in the divine power of the stylites that their columns had to be fenced off to prevent pilgrims chipping off bits of stone as relics, thereby endangering the life of the occupant. How disturbing it must have been for a stylite to hear the clink of chisels at work on the base on his column! Additional security was provided by a companion who sought to keep the crowds under control; he also supplied the stylite with his meagre food requirements which were usually placed in a basket lowered on the end of a rope. The companion also had charge of the ladder which was occasionally raised for visitors to ascend to the stylite for personal interviews on the top of the column.

When a stylite died, his body and clothes were prized as sacred relics and the fierce desire to possess them led to some hideous incidents. Some years prior to the death of Simeon there was a fierce battle over the body of St Maron who lived on the mountain of Qala'at Kalota, and the hermit Salmana near the Euphrates was twice carried off when close to death by those avid relic collectors who could not restrain their impatience. As for Simeon himself, by far the richest prize of all, his body was immediately claimed by the Patriarch of Antioch who arrived on the spot in the company of six bishops and several hundred soldiers. The deceased was paraded in triumph to Antioch where the

crowds waited, candles in hand. Simeon's body was deposed firstly in the
Church of Cassianus and then a month later transferred to Constantine's great
church where it was considered as the city's greatest treasure and a sure protection against invaders, earthquakes and the plague. But such a relic could not
long escape the attention of Constantinople, which eventually overrode the
opposition of Antioch and removed Simeon to the capital of Byzantium.

Deprived of Simeon's mortal remains, the monks at Telanissos made his
column the central point for a vast octagonal area on which four enormous
basilicas converged to provide a covered space capable of holding about 10,000
pilgrims. The monastery at the foot of the hill became the centre of a burgeoning
pilgrimage commerce, with hospices and shops catering for the needs of the
visitors. From here the *via sacra* led up the hill to the great church itself. The
ruins of Qala'at Sama'an, as they are now known, still convey the majestic
beauty of the original building constructed in the fifth and sixth centuries; but to
complete the picture one must imagine the endless throng of pilgrims which
must have made the place as popular as Lourdes is today.

Simeon has achieved international renown as the stylite saint, but the honour
of patron saint of Syria fell to the unlikely person of Sergius who was one of the
last of the Christian martyrs. In 305, only eight years before Christianity was to
be legalised by the Edict of Milan, a commander of the guard by the name of
Sergius was convicted as a Christian and brought to Resafa in eastern Syria to
receive his punishment. Apparently, the Roman authorities wished to make a
special example of him as a lesson to other potential Christians in the imperial
ranks. Sergius arrived for his execution in the desert outpost of Resafa in a
shocking state, having been forced to make the twenty-six kilometre march from
the Euphrates in shoes lined with sharp nails. He was led to his death by a rope
passed through a hole bored in his lips, although, as a Roman citizen, he was
permitted the luxury of decapitation by the sword. And there the story of the
unfortunate Sergius might have ended had not his gruesome martyrdom
become a *cause célèbre*.

Although Resafa was an isolated spot it lay at the junction of two major
caravan routes and news of the hideous death of Sergius soon spread in all
directions. His memory was kept alive, and with the end of the persecution of
Christians a cult was established to venerate him. So strong were the feelings
aroused by the putting to death of the soldier Sergius that the place of his
martyrdom was renamed Sergiopolis* and a small church built to mark his grave.

*The city as it can be seen today was built by the Ghassanids, a Christianised Arab tribe.

In the early fifth century a great basilica and a monastery were constructed inside the walls of the town. By 550 the basilica had been promoted to a cathedral and Sergiopolis was the centre of four subordinate bishoprics. This meteoric rise in importance was greatly aided by the lucrative revenue accruing from the pilgrimage traffic, but the most impressive physical aspect of this transformation of a desert outpost to a thriving township lay in the organisation of a water supply adequate to meet the needs of the growing population. The full technical resources of Byzantium were summoned in support of the new settlement. The vast brick vaults of the water cisterns are as majestic a sight as any at Sergiopolis; it is like peering down into a series of subterranean cathedral naves.

Possibly the rulers in Constantinople saw here a convenient opportunity to put religious fervour to the service of the military requirements, to establish an obstacle to the Sassanian threat in the east. But, whatever the motive behind the creation of Sergiopolis, the Byzantine achievement commands respect. From a distance, the town appears almost intact behind its walls of glinting white gypsum. These extensive fortifications form a rough rectangle measuring approximately 550 metres × 410 × 535 × 350 and contain some fifty defensive towers. Four gates give access to the town, of which the north gate leading to the Euphrates is the most richly decorated and is one of the town's principal sights. Its frieze of grapes and vine leaves and its acanthus capitals evoke the image of a greener, more fertile environment than is encountered today. By contrast, the decoration of the basilica tends towards simplicity. This building was the third resting place of St Sergius, following an earthquake which caused great damage to the martyry itself. Although little remains of this structure the fine decoration of the south apse gives a powerful idea of the original splendour. The area enclosed within the mighty walls was once covered with houses and streets laid out in the manner of the early Seleucid cities; now, nothing can be seen but a series of mounds partly overgrown with rough desert grass. The desolation is complete.

That the Christian faith in Syria was able to raise such monuments as Sergiopolis and Qala'at Sama'an was due to the widespread religious fervour of the time. It has already been noted that, by his example, St Simeon founded a movement of stylite monks who mounted columns all over the Near East and Asia Minor in order to proclaim the glories of Christ. The fashion even spread to Europe for a while but was stopped by the church authorities, who deemed the practice unsuitable in view of the climate. In Syria, however, the stylites were greeted with unreserved enthusiasm; novices were rigorously tested before being allowed to adopt the life of a stylite, but once aloft they became the special pride of the monasteries which catered for their practical needs. Indeed, a stylite did much to enhance the reputation of a monastery and the disciples of a stylite might in themselves form the basis for a future community of monks. There was thus a great measure of interdependence between the organised monastic society and the lone stylites on their columns. However, such intimate relations with the world at large would have seemed abhorrent to certain other practitioners of asceticism who roamed the countryside and desert of Syria in those early days of Christianity.

St Jerome is a famous example of an ascetic who left his monastery, tired of the petty theological bickering of the other monks, and withdrew to a life of solitude in the Syrian desert. Having endured the hardships of this self-imposed exile and attained thereby a state of mystical enlightenment, Jerome pursued his career as a saintly writer and served for a while as secretary to the Pope in Rome. He evidently held a balanced view of the ascetic way of life, for he recorded his strong disapproval of the excesses of those who showed a suspicious leaning towards ostentation. Asceticism was a common phenomenon in Syria in Jerome's day: all over the country hermits were seeking solitary retreats in huts, caves, cisterns, towers and even in tombs and tree trunks. These 'athletes of virtue' avoided contact – as far as was possible – with human society, which they felt had lost its true religious vocation. The forms of their asceticism were numerous, with each individual devising and improvising his own methods of self-mortification. Some would remain standing on one spot year after year, others would shun the call of sleep and keep themselves in a constant state of vigilance, and still others would go about on all fours like animals and live from a diet of roots, leaves, fruit and berries. In some cases, washing was dispensed with, and there must have been some forlorn and repulsive human beings wandering the land in torn rags and filthy animal-skins, their emaciated limbs covered with boils and sores and their hair hanging in long tresses thickly matted with dirt. It was this form of asceticism which Jerome criticised as ostentatious behaviour. Yet these 'mad-men of God' were by all accounts strongly motivated by an earnestness of faith. Drawn mainly from simple country stock and speaking Syriac rather than Greek, their lives demonstrated an attempt to practise the literal message of the Gospels and to find in solitude and contemplation an immediate experience of the absolute nature of God.

What drove St Jerome into the desert from the relative comfort of his monk's cell at Chalcis was partly the endless theological disputations in which his companions indulged. Indeed, the fervour of early Christianity in Syria was matched only by its fanatical disagreements over fine points of doctrine involving the true nature of God and Christ. The Council of Nicaea (AD 325), which gave Christians the Nicene Creed, was already deeply concerned with the question of heresy and condemned Arianism as a doctrine which, by separating the persons of the Trinity in a hierarchy, tended to deny the divinity of Christ. There was, however, no shortage of new heresies to occupy the hearts and minds of the authorities and the people; this was particularly so in Syria where the official views of Byzantium were usually opposed, partly out of a sense of national awakening. Alienation from the rulers in Constantinople was indeed rife in spite of the meticulous administration which promoted prosperity, for the dual burden of heavy taxation and a leaden bureaucracy lay upon the province.

Although nationalism played its part, the spirit of theological controversy had a life of its own in Syria during the fourth and fifth centuries. The main cause of dissension continued to centre on the true nature of Christ and other related details. Following the condemnation of Arianism at Nicaea, Apollinaris, Bishop of Laodicea, presented in around 390 the new concept that Christ, while having the body and soul of a man, had the 'Logos' or Word of God as his spirit. This idea was further refined by Nestorius, who held that in Christ were joined in perfect harmony of action the divine and the human. This view was later condemned at the Council of Ephesus in 431. The last great schism of the oriental church, known as Monophysitism, rejected the doctrine of the two natures and proclaimed simply that the human and the divine in Christ were completely joined within the unity of a single nature. This was repudiated by the Council of Chalcedon in 451 and the stage was set for a long and bitter controversy which sapped the energy of the young Christian faith.

Syria was generally behind the thesis of the Monophysites, who claimed St Simeon as a backer of their cause; but at Antioch there was considerable support for the doctrine of the dual nature propounded by the Council of Chalcedon. The religious division followed roughly the national division between those Hellenised members of town society, who took the official view, and the broad masses of Syriac speakers in the countryside. In Antioch there were simultaneously two patriarchs of the contending schools of doctrine; and it has been postulated that the large number of churches in the 'Dead Cities' can be partly ascribed to the need for separate places of worship for the divided communities of Monophysites and Chalcedonians. The rivalry between the two factions sometimes adopted more violent expression and on more than one occasion the quarrel degenerated into bloody conflict. In 517 a group of several hundred monks from Apamea (pro-Council of Chalcedon), on a pilgrimage to the column of St Simeon, were attacked by a horde of Monophysites, who massacred 350 of their number.

Antioch was, nevertheless, at the heart of a tremendous spiritual renewal and its churchmen included those of the calibre of John Chrysostom (347–407), the 'golden-mouth', noted for his gifts as a preacher. Abandoning his prescribed career as a lawyer for the life of an ascetic on a mount near the city, Chrysostom returned charged with a spiritual energy to fulminate against the lax morals and luxurious living of the citizens of Antioch. As an early version of Luther, Calvin and Knox he singled out the rich and powerful for special criticism. His promotion in 398 as Patriarch of Constantinople proved to be his undoing. His comparison of Eudoxia, wife of Arcadius, to Herodias was the immediate cause of his banishment but one suspects that his radical views did not endear him to the ecclesiastical establishment. John Chrysostom met his death probably as a result of exhaustion, on the long march into exile in the Caucasus which he was forced to undertake. His eloquent sermons and outspoken honesty assure his place as one of the leading and most respected teachers of Christian ethics of all time.

The great religious and economic expansion of Syria in the fourth to sixth centuries took place under the constant threat of attack and invasion from the Sassanians in the east, who clashed with Byzantium throughout the entire Near East. At first, led by Belisarius during the reign of Justinian, the Byzantine forces were able to inflict defeat on the Sassanians in their own territory; but soon Syria lay helpless at the feet of the invaders under Chosroes I (531–79). In 540 the Sassanians advanced again and, although Sergiopolis held out, Aleppo was put to flames and Antioch thoroughly sacked. The cathedral of Antioch was stripped of its treasures, the town destroyed and its inhabitants taken into captivity. This disaster followed the great earthquake of 526 in which as many as a quarter of a million inhabitants of Antioch are said to have perished. These two catastrophic events marked the end of Antioch's intellectual, economic and political pre-eminence. Before withdrawing, Chosroes proceeded to extort large ransoms from Apamea and Chalcis. A truce was agreed in 542 which brought some respite, but at the beginning of the seventh century the Sassanians, now under Chosroes II, descended once more on Syria. This time they sacked Damascus and made off with the relic of the true cross from the Church of the Holy Sepulchre in Jerusalem which they left in ruins.

Under the leadership of Heraclius, Byzantium had enough strength to strike back and restore the cross to Jerusalem in 629; but this tug-of-war over Syria was overtaken by the Arab-Islamic expansion which, bursting forth from Arabia into the lands of the Fertile Crescent, carried all before it. Only five years after the triumph of Heraclius over the Sassanians, Damascus surrendered to the forces of Islam. Syria was set for another phase of religious renewal during the glorious founding years of the first Muslim dynasty under the Umayyad caliphate. For all its power and organisation, Byzantium was forced to abandon Syria to the rampant desert warriors, whose battle cry 'There is no God but God' dispensed with all the proposals and counter-proposals of Nestorians, Monophysites and Chalcedonians at a stroke.

Reckoned in terms of years, Syria's experience as a wholly Christian country was of short duration, a mere three centuries extending from the 'Peace of the Church' in 313 until the Muslim conquest of 636. However, in contrast to the beliefs of previous civilisations in Syria, Christianity has survived until the present day. The great church and convent at Sednaya and the Aramaic-speaking Christian community at Ma'aloula, where the language of Christ can still be heard as the current vernacular, are living witnesses to the enduring vigour of the Christian faith in Syria. In Aleppo and Damascus churches and mosques co-exist as close neighbours. Although the original Church of St John the Baptist now lies beneath the Umayyad Mosque in Damascus, Christian places of worship have come through the ages remarkably unscathed and include country churches, monasteries, convents and shrines.

In historical terms, Syria's role in the establishment and propagation of early Christianity can hardly be overstated. At a time when most of Europe was pagan and living in the Dark Ages, Syrian missionaries and merchants were carrying the new faith of Christianity on their journeys throughout the known world. At the same time Syrian architects and craftsmen were erecting monuments to the Christian faith which would not be equalled in Europe for several hundred years. It is thus not without irony that Christian Europe in the Middle Ages was to launch a Holy War against the very country which had helped Christianity through its birth pains.

The Monuments of Syria

Winged sun-disc from Tell Halaf, supported by two Sumero-Babylonian figures. Enkidu, half-man, half-bull, is represented twice in mirror image. Syro-Hittite, ninth century BC.

Alabaster statue with encrusted eyes from Temple of Ishtar, Mari, representing an unknown youth. The hands are clasped in a typical gesture of piety and adoration – such votive statues were placed beside statues of the gods.

Entrance to Ugarit, a Canaanite city of the second and third millennia BC.

View of Tell Mardikh, site of the great city of Ebla. Excavated since 1964, it has revealed evidence of a native Syrian civilisation in the second and third millennia BC.

The mysterious cella at Amrit, sitting in a sacred pool, is an enigmatic testimony to the religious beliefs of the Phoenicians.

Palmyra – a general view of the ruins, with the theatre in the foreground.

Fallen masonry at Palmyra shows the high quality of the carving, using naturalistic foliage patterns (above).

Entrance to the main street of Palmyra. The angled arch disguises the bend in the street (left).

Palmyrene funerary sculpture displayed in the museum, Palmyra. The carvings are famous for their characteristic frontal style.

Superb limestone funerary sculpture from one of the tower tombs at Palmyra (above).

Detail of carving at the Temple of Baal, Palmyra – one of a series of bas-reliefs which adorned the beams of the temple. The moon-god, Aglibol, is standing by an altar on which are lying pomegranates and pine cones (left).

The magnificent Roman theatre at Bosra, now partially restored, gives an idea of the sophisticated civilisation of the Hauran plain in the south of Syria. In the Islamic period the theatre was enclosed within a formidable fortification.

The basilica of St Simeon. The stump of the stylite's column, once sixty feet high, is the focal point of the great structure built to commemorate the saint.

Byzantine fortifications at Halabiya, an outpost on the Euphrates. These were built by the Emperor Justinian as a defence against the Sassanians, who later destroyed the city.

Resafa, originally known as Sergiopolis, grew up around the shrine of a Christian martyr, the Roman soldier Sergius, who was put to death in AD 305. The best preserved architectural feature is the richly decorated north gate.

The 'Dead Cities', comprising numerous chapels and churches as well as farms and houses, are an early Christian architectural heritage unique to Syria. Here are shown churches at Burg Haydar (left) and Mushabak (right). The detail of carving around the windows is particularly fine.

Part of the famous Barada panel, an eighth-century Umayyad mosaic in the Great Mosque, Damascus (above).

The facade of the Umayyad castle of Qasr al-Hayr al-Gharbi, now partially reconstructed, decorates the main entrance of the National Museum of Antiquities, Damascus (left).

Mosaic facade, partially restored, in the Great Mosque, Damascus (overleaf).

The legendary Crusader castle of Krak des Chevaliers. The high-quality masonry is in an excellent state of preservation.

Saladin's Castle, one of the most dramatic strongholds in Syria, is protected by a twenty-five-metre deep channel, hewn out of the rock. It was captured by Salah al-Din (Saladin) in 1188, a year after his decisive victory at Hittin.

The Citadel at Aleppo owes its present appearance to the Ayyubids and Mamluks, but it was an occupied stronghold for thousands of years previously.

The Madrasa al-Firdous in Aleppo, founded in 1233, is one of the finest creations of the Ayyubid period (right).

*Nassan House in Damascus, showing the traditional features of the courtyard with fountain and 'liwan'
seating area (above).*

*Achikbache House in Aleppo is the finest of the city's eighteenth-century courtyard houses, noted for rich
stone carving around the windows. It now serves as the Museum of Local Folklore (right).*

Khan Asad Pasha, the greatest of the surviving caravanserais in Damascus, was completed around the end of the eighteenth century. The upper floor housed the merchants (above).

Al-Azm Palace, Damascus, the most sumptuous private dwelling in the city, was built around 1749 and is now a museum (left).

The mosque of Khalid ibn al-Walid, Homs. This building dates back only to the early twentieth century, although it contains the shrine of the great seventh-century Islamic general.

The Umayyads and the Dawn of Islam

At the beginning of the seventh century, Syria was a solidly Christian country, despite some pagan elements surviving especially in remote areas, and was still under the political control of the Byzantine Empire. However, the hold and protection of Constantinople had become tenuous. During 611–14 Chosroes II had led the Sassanian army on a campaign of pillage and destruction through Syria, looting Damascus and murdering or taking captive its population. During the period immediately prior to the dawning of the Islamic era in 622, Syria appeared to be morally and materially in a state of decline. However, it would be a mistake to overstate the economic and cultural slump caused by the rampaging of the Sassanians, for the imminent flowering of the country under the Islamic caliphate of the Umayyads was to reach such heights in such a short time that it must be assumed that Syria had been lying dormant rather than destroyed. Indeed, the vigour of Syria was still sufficiently intact for the country to make a decisive contribution to nascent Islam.

Islam, the third and final of the revealed religions of the Middle East, came from the same mould as its predecessors, Judaism and Christianity: a message was transmitted through the person of a prophet in the wilderness. Yet Mohammed, unlike Jesus, did not claim to be divine, simply the messenger chosen by Allah. Thus it was not Mohammed but the message in the form of the Quran which Islam considered to be holy. Accordingly, the literal meaning of the original text, as revealed in the language of Mohammed, contained not only the essence of the new religion but came to stand as a symbol of Allah in the most concrete manner. To the new community of the believers Islam meant, literally, submission to the word of Allah as revealed in the Quran. The central message, despite the many complex matters which are treated, was of a stunning simplicity and can be summarised in the affirmation: 'There is no God but Allah and Mohammed is his Prophet'. In fact a more accurate translation of the Arabic would be simply: 'There is no God but God'. Allah was not understood as a deity belonging to a pantheon containing other deities, nor even as a God bearing any resemblance to the humans He had created. Nor could it be maintained that Allah was the sum of the universe, but rather that the universe was in Him. This is not to suggest that the first Muslims were adepts of theological method. On the contrary, Allah was beyond understanding and certainly beyond the realm of discussion. The first converts to Islam were Arabian tribesmen whose creed was the simple but passionate belief that Allah *is*, and that the words of the Quran are His own, summing up the whole of His message to mankind. From this it can be seen that the possibility of speculation on the nature of Allah was inconceivable from the outset. There was absolutely no room in Islam for the equivalents of the Nestorians and Monophysites; Islam's religious schisms were to come about as a result of disagreements over the more practical issue of succession to the authority of the Prophet. And these were not long in coming to a head.

The birth of Islam dates from Mohammed's *hijrah* or migration from Mecca, where the message was not initially accepted, to Yathrib; this latter was renamed 'Medinat al-Nabi', i.e. the town of the Prophet, and is now known simply as Medina. It is from this year, 622 in the Gregorian calendar, that the Muslim era officially begins, and this is by no means an arbitrary date, since the support of the people of Medina was a crucial event in the spreading of Islam. Mohammed's house in Medina formed both the first headquarters and the principal place of worship of the new religion. From this humble base, the message of Allah was carried by the newly converted desert tribes, and submission to Allah was often achieved with the threat or use of military force. During the lifetime of the Prophet this proselytising consisted of little more than sporadic incursions and only the southernmost part of Syria was affected. After Mohammed's death in 632 the work was continued by the first two caliphs, or successors, Abu-Bakr (632–4) and Umar (634–44), and gradually assumed the dimensions of an organised expansion.

There were also underlying socio-economic causes behind the Arabian Islamic expansion, and the northward thrust of the tribes was in the tradition of the great Semitic migrations of the Amorites, Canaanites and Aramaeans. Nevertheless, the banner of Islam was more than a pretext covering territorial ambitions and dreams of an easy life in the relatively lush pastures of the Fertile Crescent. There was a new approach to the business of conquest and to the treatment of the subjugated peoples, which stands in marked contrast to the sackings and massacres previously suffered by the Syrians. The victorious general of the Islamic forces, Khalid ibn al-Walid, exemplified this when he appeared unexpectedly in the rear of the Byzantine army in 635 and received the surrender of Damascus on terms which must have seemed unbelievable to the beleaguered inhabitants of the city. According to historical tradition, he proclaimed: 'In the name of Allah, the Compassionate, the Merciful. This is what Khalid ibn al-Walid would grant to the inhabitants of Damascus if he enters therein: he promises to give them security for their lives, property and churches. Their city wall shall not be demolished, neither shall any Moslem be quartered in their houses. Thereunto we give to them the pact of Allah and the protection of His Prophet, the caliphs and the believers. So long as they pay the poll tax, nothing but good shall befall them.' The practical benefits of this policy of tolerance and magnanimity in victory were soon to become apparent, but the career of Khalid ibn al-Walid ended at the moment of his triumph over the Byzantine forces. Following a successful conclusion to the military conquest of Syria, the caliph Umar implemented a policy switch requiring administrators rather than generals. Relieved of his duties, Khalid ibn al-Walid retired to a life of anonymity in the city of Homs, where he died in 642. The magnificent shrine and mosque in Homs were erected in his memory as recently as 1908.

The consolidation of the Islamic presence in Syria proceeded according to a set of principles which have come to be known as the 'covenant' of Umar. The Christians were not encouraged to embrace Islam, partly because as nonbelievers they were taxable, but also because the Arabian Muslims in the early stages of the Islamic expansion felt that their religion and ethnic or tribal identity were somehow an exclusive property which it would be unwise to amalgamate with foreign peoples. Thus we have the strange situation in Syria during the early years of Islam of the militant believers in Allah living in peaceful condominium with the Christians and seeking to play the role of a type of religio-military aristocracy. Furthermore, Muslims debarred themselves from holding land other than that which was abandoned, and even that would be held in the name of the community rather than of individuals. Possibly this was to discourage the sedentarisation of the tribes who were needed for the continuation of the Islamic conquests west into Egypt and North Africa and east into Mesopotamia and Persia. During this second phase of the expansion, Syria served as the hub, although Mecca was still the seat of the caliphate. Yet perhaps the most significant aspect of the conquest of Syria was that the country was a rich and sophisticated centre of civilisation and it 'gave the nascent power of Islam prestige before the world and confidence in itself' *.

Meanwhile, events in the Hijaz[†], the heartland of Islam, were taking shape in a way which would soon have a spectacular outcome for the province of Syria. The dispute over the rightful successor to the authority of the Prophet divided those who favoured the principle of direct descent through Ali, who was both cousin to Mohammed and husband to his daughter Fatima, from those who viewed the caliphate as a temporal leadership best served by the selection of the most suitable candidate from the tribe of the Prophet, the Quraysh. The intricacies of the dispute, and of the resulting split into the pro-Ali or Shi'ite faction and the Sunnites, need not concern us here. Of significance is the assassination of the caliph Uthman (644–56) by alleged supporters of Ali, who then declared Ali caliph in the place of the deceased. Only Muawiya, a cousin of Uthman and also the governor of Syria, refused to swear allegiance to the new caliph. Instead, he called on Ali to punish the guilty or take the guilt upon himself. In the circumstances this demand for application of tribal justice amounted to a challenge to the caliphate itself. Battle was duly joined in 657 and Muawiya is reported to have avoided defeat by the device of attaching Qurans to the lances of his cavalry, as if summoning divine arbitration to decide the outcome. The issue remained unresolved, however, until 661 when Ali was assassinated in al-Kufah by one of his original supporters. Muawiya was then proclaimed caliph and, making Damascus his official residence, he ushered in that most auspicious period in the history of Syria and of early Islam, known after the name of the founding dynasty as the Umayyad caliphate. It lasted less than a century, from 661 until 750, but has left more vivid memories than the previous millennium of Seleucid, Roman and Byzantine rule.

Muawiya proved more than worthy of the founder-role he played as the first of the Umayyad caliphs. His policy of reconciliation with the Christians left the administration of state in the hands of experienced men. The bureaucracy was even extended to include a system of registry and the rudiments of a postal service. His approach to the human dimension of wielding power showed the gentle wisdom of experience. It is recorded that he once said, 'I apply not my

*Hitti, *History of Syria*.
[†]The area of Saudi Arabia where Mecca and Medina are located.

sword where my lash suffices; nor my lash, where my tongue is enough. And even if there be one hair binding me to my fellow men, I do not let it break. When they pull, I loosen; and if they loosen I pull.' Muawiya's political sureness of touch was instrumental in laying the foundations of the secular state of Islam, but this did not endear him to the supporters of Ali who now campaigned for the caliphate to pass to the direct descendants of Ali's union with Fatima.

The mood of the early years of the Umayyads under Muawiya must have been one of pre-occupation with the need to consolidate power and to appease the enemies of yesterday. For all his qualities of statesmanship and system-building Muawiya left behind no architectural monuments to his reign. There is testimony of his residence in Damascus in the 'Green Palace', probably a domed structure, but no traces of this remain. Perhaps the new regime still lacked the confidence to express its authority in terms of stone buildings, but this architectural reticence can also be ascribed to the fact that the Umayyads brought with them from Arabia no architectural tradition. Creswell perhaps was overstating the case when he described Arabia in the seventh century as 'an almost perfect architectural vacuum' *, but the fact remains that the vernacular building style of the Hijaz did not possess the technical skills to raise such monuments as the victorious Arabs now found in their new territory of Syria. Their reaction to the great buildings of Rome and Byzantium was, in the words of Oleg Grabar, 'one of awe and admiration'[†]. There was a vast cultural gap to be bridged and neither Muawiya nor his immediate successors were ready for the task. It was not until the rule of Abd al-Malik (685–705) and his son al-Walid (705–15) that the Umayyads began to apply their creative energies to the business of architecture; their first achievement was no less than the erection in 691–2 of the Dome of the Rock in Jerusalem which was commissioned by Abd al-Malik to impress on the community of the believers the shift in the power centre of Islam away from the Hijaz to Syria and Palestine. Perhaps as a visible act of piety the original mosque at the house of the Prophet in Medina was rebuilt in a more worthy manner, but there was no mistaking that the Umayyads had succeeded in drawing the focus of attention onto themselves and onto Syria.

Al-Walid continued what his father had begun. The construction of the Great Mosque at Damascus between 705 and 714 was his first and most ambitious

*Creswell, *Early Muslim Architecture*.
[†]Grabar, *The Formation of Islamic Art*.

undertaking upon succeeding to the caliphate in 705. It is worth taking a close look at the history and construction of this great building since it raises questions which go straight to the heart of the origins and inspiration of early Islamic art. During the years 636–705 the ancient Roman Temple of Damascene Jupiter, which itself possibly stood on the site of an earlier shrine to Hadad, the lord of storm and lightning, was shared by the Muslim and Christian communities of Damascus. Whether or not the temple itself had been demolished or merely converted into a Christian church is uncertain and the exact nature of this partitioning between the two faiths has caused a great deal of confusion and controversy. Some have interpreted the sharing to relate to the church building itself but the view now accepted is that it concerned the actual inner courtyard of the temple, and that the Cathedral of St John almost certainly stood in the middle towards the western end of the courtyard. Thus the entire church fell within the half allotted to the Christians while the Muslims took the eastern half, which probably contained no buildings at all. This apparent disadvantage would not have posed a great problem to early Muslims since the concept of the mosque was of a space in which to gather for prayer, rather than of a specific building as such.

Thus we can visualise the situation at the beginning of the eighth century, with the ancient enclosing wall of the Temple of Damascene Jupiter, a fine construction of limestone masonry measuring approximately 160 by 100 metres along its outer circumference, providing a vast courtyard, a majestic setting for the Cathedral of St John. Perhaps the Muslims had a hypostyle structure, familiar from Medina, in order to provide some measure of shelter. This would probably have been a humble affair next to the Byzantine church (or indeed the converted temple), underlining the stark contrast between the simplicity of the new Arabian faith and the technical and artistic sophistication of Christianity at that time. Be that as it may, Islam was now poised to create a grandiose expression of its own and to challenge Christianity in terms of architecture. In 705 al-Walid offered to buy the church from the Christians and according to Arab historians this is how he took possession of it.

It is significant that al-Walid did not seek – as had hitherto been the practice of his ancestors in Syria – to convert the church into a mosque. Clearly, Islam had come of age under the Umayyads and was now ready for its own works. An ambition to outdo the Christians is reported by the tenth-century Arab chronicler al-Muqaddasi: 'For he beheld Syria to be a country that had long been occupied by Christians, and he noted therein the beautiful churches still belonging to them, so enchantingly fair, and so renowned for their splendour ... So he sought to build for the Muslims a mosque that should prevent their regarding these, and that should be unique and a wonder to the world.' Accordingly, al-Walid ordered the demolition of the church and the construction of the Great Mosque. Memory of the Christian church survives in a solitary Greek inscription on the south side of the outer wall. It reads: 'Thy Kingdom, O Christ, is an everlasting Kingdom, and Thy dominion endureth throughout all generations.' There is no trace of the exact location of the earlier church-cum-temple and, short of excavating beneath the courtyard of the Great Mosque itself, this is likely to remain a matter of speculation. More importantly, it now stands proven beyond reasonable doubt that the Umayyad Mosque was not a conversion of the Christian church but was a new Islamic foundation, and one which certainly lived up to the expectations of al-Walid; mediaeval Muslims acclaimed it as one of the wonders of the world and even today it ranks among the most impressive buildings of all ages.

Al-Walid cleared the entire courtyard, leaving only the Roman walls and towers, and along the entire length of the south wall he built the Great Mosque. It was a vast rectangular building, consisting of three equal aisles divided between two rows of arches; the arches were mounted on columns with Corinthian capitals and provided a covered space of 136 by 36 metres. The three parallel 'naves' were crossed mid-way by a transversal and a dome was mounted over the point of intersection. The south wall thus became the *qibla*, the term designating the direction of Mecca and the orientation for prayer. Accordingly the congregation stood facing the long south wall at prayer-time. The remainder of the space was used as an open courtyard of 120 by 50 metres, with one side flanking the mosque and an arcade with columns surrounding the other three sides. In this dramatically simple manner the existing space was redeployed to meet the new requirements of the Islamic faith.

It has already been noted that the Umayyads did not bring with them an architectural model or any Islamic prototype from Arabia – if one excepts the Prophet's house at Medina – and neither did they have a defined attitude to architecture at the time. It was in Syria that Islam was confronted with the challenge of expressing itself in terms of the available Greco-Roman and Byzantine vocabulary of building; and the answer to that challenge was formulated entirely within the technical and artistic repertoire of the existing Syrian tradition. It was quite literally within the framework offered by the Roman courtyard and using the skills of the local builders that the Islamic ideal in architecture defined itself through a totally novel distribution of space. The focus of attention was no longer a shrine or altar but the space itself, in which the community of the believers gathered for prayer.

The Umayyad Mosque in Damascus can be said almost to have shaped the Islamic attitude or approach to the design of all mosques, for it became one prototype which, along with one or two others, contained all the basic elements which were imitated throughout the expanding Islamic territory. Furthermore, it was in Damascus that the idea of the minaret evolved from the use of the Roman towers in order to give the call to prayer. Although the minaret has become a design feature of Islamic architecture, the new organisation of space constitutes the essence. The most immediate impression of the Umayyad Mosque is the striking aspect of a vast space stretching away. Inside there are hundreds of brightly coloured carpets and the barest minimum in furniture. Outside there is the great courtyard which is a novel experience for the Westerner accustomed to seeing architecture as individual buildings to be contemplated for their intrinsic value. Around three sides of the courtyard there is a minimum of building, just enough to contain and hold the space without appearing to impinge on it. This triumph in the art of spatial organisation has survived the vandalism of history which destroyed almost all of the original ornamentation of the building.

But to complete the picture, it is necessary to consider the lavish embellishment of the structure. Fragments of glass mosaic decorate the space between the arches and above the columns, and below them some panels of marble serve to recall that the Umayyad Mosque was at the time of its construction a vibrantly and richly adorned edifice throughout. Fortunately, the little that has survived is sufficient for us to visualise the original splendour described by eye-witness accounts such as that of al-Muqaddasi in the tenth century: 'The Mosque is the most beautiful thing Muslims possess in our time. We know of no other of their treasures that can surpass it. In the golden parts of the mosaics figure trees, capital cities, and inscriptions of the greatest beauty and delicacy, and of exquisite workmanship.' Ibn Battuta, passing through Damascus in 1326, commented: 'The Cathedral Mosque, known as the Umayyad Mosque, is the most magnificent mosque in the world, the finest in construction and noblest in beauty, grace and perfection.'

Ibn Battuta was most struck by the marble panels but it is generally held that the mosaics created the most vivid and lasting impression. Above all the famous Barada panel, which had been plastered over at an undetermined date during the Turkish occupation of Syria and was uncovered during 1927–9, was reckoned to be 'one of the most important discoveries of our time in the realm of the

History of Art'. The words are those of Marguerite van Berchem, whose personal intervention led to the 'excavation' of the mosaics. The thrill of the return to view of a vast panel measuring 34.5 by 7.15 metres is apparent in her account:

> 'From under the huge slabs of plaster which were removed from the walls without difficulty and which fell to the ground in clouds of white dust, a most fairy-like decoration came to light: fantastic and varied architecture, from towns with classical buildings, of which prototypes, more conventional and less varied, are found on Roman frescoes, to cities of the East with their clusters of cupolas, evoking, according to eyewitnesses of the Middle Ages, the most renowned places of pilgrimage; slender kiosks with leafy roofs, reminiscent perhaps of the hunting-boxes where the Umayyad Khalifs enjoyed resting after the hunt in the cool of their gardens and fountains. Trees are also depicted with flexible branches laden with golden fruit, sometimes in rows on the edge of a river, sometimes following the curves of the arched portico of the court. This river, which ancient writers identified with the Barada, flows bubbling along the whole length of more than 34 metres at the bottom of the great panel we are describing, its azure and silver waters rushing now and again under a single-arched bridge.' *

The re-appearance of the Barada panel helped rekindle an old controversy. Ibn Battuta, among other chroniclers, passed on the story that none other than the Christian Emperor of Byzantium had despatched workers to complete the mosque and its decoration. His version reads: 'The person who undertook its construction was the caliph Walid I. He applied to the Roman Emperor at Constantinople, ordering him to send craftsmen to him, and the Emperor sent him twelve thousand of them.' The more reliable al-Muqaddasi, writing in *c*985, reported only of Copts from Egypt and Greeks from Syria being hired for the project, although materials did come partly from Byzantium. Furthermore, we learn that it cost seven years 'land tax', i.e. the revenue from the whole of Syria, to defray the expense of the work.

---

*The Barada is the river of Damascus. M. van Berchem's account appears in Creswell's *Early Muslim Architecture*.

Given the political situation at the time – the Umayyads had just chased the Byzantines from Syria and were now carrying the war into their own territory – it seems hardly likely that the Christian Emperor would have felt disposed to provide such technical and cultural assistance for a major Islamic monument that symbolised his defeat. However, Byzantine participation at an unofficial level is almost certain. At the time of the construction of the Umayyad Mosque the Muslims still represented a small minority in the population and there would probably have been no shortage of Christian craftsmen, Syrianised Greeks, especially in Damascus, available to be hired or conscripted for the work. That the skills employed were derived from the civilisation of Byzantium is beyond doubt; but from an art-historical point of view it is not just a matter of the origin of the craftsmen but also of the creative inspiration which guided their technical efforts.

The absence of human figures – perhaps the most obvious feature of the mosaics in general and of the Barada panel in particular – is of course to be ascribed to the Islamic avoidance of representation in religious art. The mosaics, while offering an exotic abundance of natural phenomena such as trees, water, hills and fields, and man-made creations such as houses, palaces, roads and bridges, are completely devoid of human life. Art historians, wishing to stress the local Syrian inspiration of the work, have identified the river with the Barada of Damascus and the trees as all being natives to the region. Others point to the account of al-Muqaddasi: 'There is hardly a tree or a famous town that has not been portrayed on these walls.' Accordingly, the Barada panel has been seen as an epic generalisation combining the triumph of Islam in various countries with a paradisiacal vision. Interesting as it is to speculate whether the Barada panel is intended as a portrait of Damascus or of the enlarged world of the Umayyad Empire, the artistic motifs can all be identified with the Syrian capital.

Religious art and architecture form but one aspect of the Umayyad achievement. Although further mosques were founded in Aleppo, Bosra, Hama and Homs, by far the greatest concentration of building was of a secular nature. In their 'cities in the desert' or 'desert palaces' the Umayyad caliphs have left a far more intimate picture of their earthly existence in a phenomenal scattering of outposts in remote areas. Though no longer nomadic, the Umayyads retained their links with the desert tribes, and appear to have used every opportunity to escape from Damascus to the open expanse of the desert steppe. Muawiya, the founder of the caliphate, sent his son Yazid to the desert bedouins in order that he might learn the noble skills of horsemanship, hunting and Arabic poetry in a language untainted by the Aramaicisms of Damascus. This atavistic yearning for the desert and all the qualities of life which it embodied have been advanced as the main reason why successive caliphs lived almost permanently outside Damascus, notably in the area known as Palmyrena. Under Hisham (724–43) this love of the desert took on a more practical form. According to Theophanes (d818): 'And he (Hisham) began to found palaces in open country and towns, and to create sown fields and gardens and to make water channels'. Resafa was to become the final resting place of the desert caliph, but his major extant monuments are the twin settlements, together known as Qasr al-Hayr.

The ruins of Qasr al-Hayr al-Gharbi (Western) lie next to the main road from Damascus to Palmyra and were thought to be of Roman origin until the excavations of 1936–8 revealed an early Islamic foundation. The site was in an advanced state of decay but the archaeologists were able to extract several important pieces of information. According to an inscription on a building which has been identified as a *khan* or caravanserai* the settlement was founded by Hisham in 727. The palace includes the tower of a Byzantine monastery which had been the previous occupant of the site, and enough remained of the twin towers of the gate and of their fantastic decoration for the ensemble to be reconstructed to form the main entrance of the National Museum in Damascus. The ground plan of the palace-cum-castle was clearly shown to have been derived from the forts of the Roman *limes*† but the manner of the Umayyad construction and the fanciful ornamentation speak more of leisure and entertainment than of any serious military function: frescoes discovered inside showed the Umayyad passion for hunting, music and drinking. This helped strengthen the notion that the installation was no more than a pleasure resort for the carefree caliph. Closer investigation of the site revealed, however, a more sophisticated infrastructure than would be required for an occasional hunting lodge or rural retreat. The settlement was linked by a 16.5-kilometre-long canal to a dam of 600 metres originally built by the Romans. The water was fed into a reservoir which supplied a mill and a cultivated area measuring some 1000 by 420 metres. Qasr al-Hayr al-Gharbi (W) was thus a working agricultural enterprise for cereal crops and not merely a princely playground. However, it was soon to be abandoned by Hisham, who was fearful of the plague and decided to move his residence even further out into the desert

Khan or caravanserai – an inn used mainly by merchants.
†*Limes* – see p. 26.

some 160 kilometres east-north-east beyond Palmyra, where there would be less risk of contact with the citizens of Damascus.

The ruins of this second settlement, Qasr al-Hayr al-Sharqi (Eastern), are far more impressive and instructive. Before this century they had been seen by many travellers, but the first proper archaeological investigation of the site was not until 1925 by Albert Gabriel. Once again Hisham left a helpful inscription: 'The construction of this town was ordered by the servant of God, Hisham, Commander of the Faithful, and this was done by the inhabitants of Homs under the direction of Sulayman ibn Ubayd in the year 110 AH[AD 728/9].' The principal remaining elements of this town have been conveniently labelled the Small Enclosure, the Large Enclosure and the Outer Enclosure. The Small Enclosure – sometimes referred to erroneously as a small castle – is the best preserved structure. Its walls are of fine limestone, which have acquired a tint variously described as amber or apricot, and form a rough square measuring seventy metres, with a series of full and semicircular towers and a monumental single-entrance gate. The inside is in ruins but it has been possible to ascertain that its function was an inn rather than a palace or castle; it is thus the earliest surviving example of a large Islamic caravanserai or *khan*. The Large Enclosure, roughly a square measuring 167 metres, is now considered to have housed the princely residence as well as the mosque, the bath-house and various other installations. Apart from the foundations and some well preserved arches and gateways there is little left to enable a picture of the place to be reconstructed.

The Outer Enclosure is truly the most enigmatic and exciting aspect of Qasr al-Hayr al-Sharqi (E). It consists of an irregular space of seven square kilometres contained within a fifteen-kilometre perimeter wall with some impressive sluice gates. Gabriel speculated that this must have formed an artificial lake; Creswell interpreted it as a huge game reserve; while Sauvaget saw above all the agricultural potential of the space and concluded that in order to understand its precise origins it was necessary to solve a problem of rural history. It was this latter agrarian approach which guided the archaeological work of Oleg Grabar on the site in the 1960s.

The published results of these excavations present a detailed picture of the ambitious scope of the settlement, which must have been a major financial investment at the time*. The hydrological works drew on a large catchment area and the water was channelled through the sluice gates into the enclosure,

*Grabar, *City in the Desert*.

thus enabling both cereal cultivation and animal grazing behind the relative security of the outer wall. This complex functioning organism, it is suggested, also fulfilled a political role for the Umayyads, permitting them to extend their control and authority over the unruly areas of Syria peopled by the nomadic tribes. Qasr al-Hayr al-Sharqi (E) was thus an exercise in nation-building and helps to explain the existence of many other similar settlements in the region through which the later Umayyads sought to organise the turbulent, nomadic elements within the new order of the Islamic state.

Thus, it would seem that the Umayyad contribution to the development of Syria was of a rural rather than an urban nature. At the beginning of the eighth century ambitious canalisation works along the Euphrates were undertaken, as well as large-scale agricultural projects in the steppe of the Jazirah*. The advance of sedentary civilisation in these areas was made possible only by the new political structure of the region. The early years of Islam turned into an area of settlement what had for a thousand years been a border zone disputed between Seleucids, Romans and Byzantines in the west, and Parthians and Sassanians in the east. Unfortunately, the 'cities in the desert' founded by the Umayyads did not outlive the end of the Umayyad caliphate by very long. With the transfer of power to the Abbasids of Iraq in 750 they were deprived of their patronage and withered away. Although Qasr al-Hayr al-Sharqi (E) was a notable exception – for the archaeological evidence shows that it was completed in early Abbasid times – the rest of the rural settlements were quickly reclaimed by the sand. Ultimately they were artificial creations of outside interests, an artificiality confirmed by the strange monumentalisation of their architecture. The mock fortifications and fanciful decoration were probably designed partly to impress the tribes with a symbol of power and partly because the Umayyads, who had no architectural notion of their own, felt that this flamboyant style was the correct thing for a princely residence.

The historical importance of the settlements at Qasr al-Hayr is nevertheless considerable, for they show a more practical aspect of the endeavours of the Umayyad princes. The image left behind by some of the later caliphs is of idle debauchery and political irresponsibility. Although most of the accounts come from sources of Abbasid propaganda it does appear that in the case of Walid II there was some substance to the reports. Walid II was not quite the end of the

*Literally 'island', denoting the triangular area in the north-east corner of Syria, between the Khabour river and the Euphrates.

line of the Umayyads for he was succeeded by the short-lived Yazid III, Ibrahim and the unfortunate Marwan II (744–50), but already the writing was on the wall. The Abbasids had managed to unite all the opposition factions and by 749 felt strong enough to proclaim the rival Abbasid caliphate at al-Kufah in Iraq. The forces of Marwan II were defeated and this last of the Umayyad caliphs escaped to Egypt where he was eventually caught and executed. Damascus was ravaged, and the Abbasids set about the extirpation of the Umayyads both dead and alive. One of the few surviving Umayyad princes, Abd al-Rahman, made a dramatic five-year trek incognito and penniless to the Islamic territory in Spain, where the glory of the Umayyads survived for another seven centuries*. Syria itself was reduced to an Abbasid province and the transfer of power and prestige from Damascus to Baghdad was relentlessly and remorselessly pursued. The white banner of the Umayyads was raised repeatedly in the years to follow but the power and the glory were henceforth with the black standard of the Abbasids.

Umayyad rule may have endured for less than a century but it was a crucial and momentous time for Syria. This was the only period in the historic era – until the founding of the present Republic – when Syria was ruled from within as a unified country. Under the Umayyads there was no governor seated in Damascus; instead the ancient city was itself the centre of power during the auspicious time when the young energies of Islam reached their furthermost extent. It was under the Umayyad caliphate that the Muslim armies carried their battles as far as Tours in France, where they were checked by Charles Martel in 732. Yet it is not primarily for their military achievement that the Umayyads are remembered. As representatives of the new religion they are noted for bringing a worldly element to the zealous puritanism of the early Islamic faith. The Umayyad condominium with the Christians was – with some minor exceptions – exemplary and without parallel. Hitti has estimated that in 732 the number of Muslims in Syria could not have exceeded 200,000 out of a total population of 3,500,000; it was, therefore, rule by persuasion as much as by coercion. Christian administrators and advisers, such as St John of Damascus, occupied the highest positions in the land. The tolerance of the Umayyads undoubtedly had practical benefits, which in the language of today would be called enlightened self-interest.

*The Umayyad prince Abd al-Rahman, son of Muawiya, was known as 'Saqr Quraish' (Hawk of Quraish). After escaping from the Abbasids to Andalusia, he founded an Umayyad state there before dying in Cordoba.

In matters of science and art the Umayyads absorbed the lessons of Greek culture and translated into Arabic a vast body of ancient knowledge. This was an essential prior step for the subsequent ninth-century Arab renaissance under the auspices of the Abbasid caliphate in Baghdad. In this great outburst of creativity it was the Syrian link which provided access to the heritage of Greek thought. In art and architecture the Umayyads had the courage to express their Islamic identity in terms of the existing sophistication of Byzantium. If they had at first been lost in awe they were certainly not overawed for long by the monuments of Greco-Roman and Christian Syria. Their novel and successful adaptation of the inherited art and architecture was a decisive step in the formation of early Islamic culture. Their 'cities in the desert' were doomed to a premature end but the technology of the water system they created for Damascus has lasted into the twentieth century.

In terms of the Syrian national consciousness the legacy of the Umayyads is also emotional and spiritual. Although Meccan in origin the Umayyads made Syria their home and gave back to the country as much as they received. Their appeal today consists of a potent mix of nostalgia for desert chivalry, a tolerant worldly attitude and Syrian glory and independence.

For historians of art and civilisation the Umayyad caliphate appears to provoke conflicting interpretations. On the one hand we are shown pre-Islamic Syria as 'a land impregnated with Hellenistic traditions, a state of affairs that was not abruptly modified' (van Berchem). On the other hand we read that 'at its thickest Hellenistic culture was only skin-deep, affecting a crust of intelligentsia in urban settlements', and that the dawning of Islam was 'a reversion to an old type, for the Arab Moslem civilisation did not introduce many original elements. It was rather a revivification of the ancient Semitic culture. Thus viewed Hellenism becomes an intrusive phenomenon between two cognate layers' (Hitti). Clearly, if Syria had absorbed enough Greek knowledge to pass on a significant contribution to the Arab renaissance then Hellenism was more than skin-deep; and if one includes the Syrian role in organised Christianity – five popes, including two saints, between 685 and 741 – then the country was probably no longer quite her old Semitic self. Yet it must be borne in mind that conflicting developments occurred in town and country which would explain such illogicalities. Whatever the truth of the matter, the fact remains that from the eighth century onwards Syria's destiny as an Arab-Islamic state was in the ascendant, and this is the identity of the country today.

The immediate aftermath of the Umayyad caliphate was a period of bloody repression instigated by the Abbasids. For Syria the accent was more on destruction than construction, as the caliphs of Baghdad sought to enhance their own territory at the expense of their neighbours. The Abbasids nevertheless left behind one major development in the city of Raqqah on the Euphrates, which was founded by al-Mansur in 772. Originally named Rafiqa, the city followed the same plan as the famous round city of Baghdad; more than half of its horseshoe-shaped walls have survived to this day. Raqqah enjoyed sufficient prestige and amenities for the caliph Harun al-Rashid to make it his official residence from 796 to 803 and it was during the ninth and tenth centuries that the city experienced its golden age. Thus the wealth and glory of the Abbasid caliphate came to rest for a while on Syrian soil, though the country as a whole did not benefit much from the occupation.

Under the Abbasids the Arabisation and Islamisation of Syria gathered pace, transforming the general Christian character of the country. The Christians were still tolerated, but their capacity to expand was contained within strict limits. Aramaic (or Syriac) gradually declined and eventually ceded place to Arabic as the vernacular of the country, which was henceforth called ash-Sham, and no longer Aram, by its inhabitants.

The Abbasid hold on Syria was loosened in the second half of the ninth century when the rival dynasty of the Tulunids (868–905) declared independence from their new base in Cairo. They were succeeded by the Ikhshids (935–69) and then the Fatimids, who during the eleventh century held the southern part of Syria while the Saljuqs of Turkestan held the north. Throughout this confusing and troubled time the only sign of independent leadership exercised from within Syria was provided by the Hamdanids, the dynasty of Hamdan who received the title Sayf al-Dawla (Sword of the State) from the Abbasid caliph and ruled from a dazzling court at Aleppo from 944 to 967. The Hamdanids were to Aleppo what the Umayyads were to Damascus; their flamboyant leadership – immortalised by the bard al-Mutanabbi – transformed briefly a provincial city into a capital of renown. Since the rule of the Hamdanids extended only to the northern part of Syria and was finished as early as 1003, their story belongs more properly to the city of Aleppo than to the country as a whole. However, the Hamdanids' continuation of the Muslim war against the might of Byzantium – which twice resulted in the temporary loss of Aleppo to the Christians in 962 and 968 and to the occupation of Antioch for over a century (968–1084) – can be viewed as a curtain-raiser for the epic struggle that was unleashed on Syrian soil at the very end of the eleventh century: the Crusades.

CHAPTER FIVE

The Legacy of the Crusades

The wars of the twelfth and thirteenth centuries between Christian Europe and the Muslim East over possession of the Holy Land were the greatest military and ideological conflict to have occurred between the two regions throughout the course of their history. Accordingly, it would indeed be surprising if Arab and European views, both contemporary and modern, were not widely divergent. The political and historical interpretation of those events, which Europe has called the Crusades, acquires a different perspective when viewed from the other side, where the designation of 'Frankish invasions' is considered more appropriate. Although it is not the purpose here to pronounce judgement, it is essential to stress that the phenomenon of the Crusades is complex, ambiguous and emotive. In order to appreciate the great stone fortresses whose ruins still decorate the Syrian landscape, a measure of the conflicting views and approaches of chroniclers and historians is required.

The European version of the Crusades begins with the fiery speech of Pope Urban II at Clermont in France on 26 November 1095. His call to 'enter upon the road to the Holy Sepulchre, wrest it from the wicked race and subject it' met with massive popular approval, best expressed in the mighty cry 'Deus le volt!', or 'God wills it!', which spread through Europe like wildfire. Thereafter, it is the standard practice of Western historians to follow the progress of the individual campaigns which are numbered for the sake of convenience from one to six. This tidy division makes little sense to the Muslims, who experienced the Crusades as a more or less continuous state of siege, whose overall pattern or logic was not apparent. There is thus from the outset a basic difference in historical method.

Hitti proposes a tripartite division of the Crusades, with the first period extending from the Frankish invasion of Antioch and Jerusalem in 1099 and the establishment of the Latin Kingdom of Jerusalem and its fiefs of Antioch, Edessa and Tripoli, until the loss of Edessa in 1144. This inaugurated the second phase, a period of Muslim recovery, initially under the Turkish Atabeg Zangi (1127–46) and his son Nur al-Din, who became master of Damascus as well as Aleppo in 1154. The unification of the Muslim world from the Nile to the Taurus and even to the Yemen was accomplished from 1171 onwards by Salah al-Din (Saladin), whose momentous victory at Hittin in 1187 over the armies of the Second Crusade led to the recapture of Jerusalem. The victories of Salah al-Din provoked the Christians to react with the prestigious Third Crusade led by Frederick Barbarossa of Germany, Philip Augustus of France and Richard Coeur de Lion of England. The battles between Richard and Salah al-Din have provided the essential legend and myth which lies at the heart of today's popular folklore. The peace treaty of 1192, which left the coast in the hands of the Latins and the interior with the Muslims, marked the end of this phase.

The third and final part covers the period from the death of Salah al-Din in 1193 to the final expulsion of the Crusaders from the mainland of Syria and Palestine one hundred years later. Petty rivalries and jealousies weakened both sides during the thirteenth century and the Muslims were subjected to the additional harassment of invasion from the east by the Mongols. Ultimate victory for the Muslims came as the Mamluks took over from the divided leadership of the Ayyubids. The defeat of the Mongols at Ain Jalut in the north of Palestine in 1260 paved the way for successful campaigns against the Crusader forces. The work was continued by Qalawun, whose death in 1290 occurred only one year before the remnant of the defeated Crusaders withdrew to the island fortress of Arwad, from which they eventually removed to Cyprus in 1303.

Viewed from Damascus, the liberation of the occupied territories must have seemed like a hollow victory when in 1300 the city, having held out against the Crusaders, was devastated by the Mongol hordes. Even more terrible was the sacking of both Damascus and Aleppo in 1400, so it is understandable that for Syria the Crusades were rapidly overshadowed by other acts of territorial aggression. Perhaps this is partly the reason why Muslim historians do not show much interest in the Crusades as an isolated historical episode: the acts of the Franks formed part of the same scenario as those of the Mongols. As Francesco Gabrieli points out in his *Arab Historians of the Crusades*, 'The Frankish invasions ... were never for the Muslim chroniclers a single subject to be treated in isolation. One would search Muslim historical writings in vain for a composite, specific History of the Wars against the Franks.' It is quite the opposite in Europe and America, where the standard works of Runciman in English, Grousset in French and Mayer in German are but the best known of a vast corpus of comprehensive studies to which new titles are being added almost every year. Clearly, the Crusades have meant more to the eventual losers and seem to be a cherished part of Europe's heritage.

Both European and Muslim accounts of the Crusades focus on the military landmarks, the battles, sieges and forced marches. Runciman's classic work *A History of the Crusades* begins on this note: 'The main theme in this volume is warfare . . . for war was the background to life in Outremer*, and the hazards of the battlefield often decided its destiny.' Against this must be set the realities of everyday life in the occupied territories and confrontation states, which are the subject of Amin Maalouf's *The Crusades through Arab Eyes*. Although the history books are cluttered with battles the occupants of the region were involved mainly with the business of daily survival and even with cultural and economic progress. The stark polarisation of the military conflict was often attenuated and obscured in the pursuit of everyday life. One might equally reverse Runciman's statement and say that peace was the background to life in Outremer, a peace which was periodically interrupted by war between Franks and Arabs, Turks and Mongols, for as long as the Crusaders maintained their claim to the Holy Places and other colonies. Life in Outremer depended indeed on the vicissitudes of war, but once the Frankish territories were established they found it lay in their own interests to co-exist with the Muslim hinterland as well as to fight it.

A peculiar relationship between Franks and Muslims came about as a result of the strange physical shape of the Frankish realm in the mid-eleventh century. The Latin Kingdom of Jerusalem, together with the County of Tripoli and the Principality of Antioch, comprised a thin strip of land nowhere more than one hundred miles across, extending from the Gulf of Aqaba in the south to the foothills of the Taurus in the north. This land was no more than a toe-hold when viewed in relation to the vast Muslim interior; its inland penetration was only fifty miles on average and sometimes less. Although the Crusaders at one time held all the ports from Latakia to Ascalon, within Syria itself the major cities of Aleppo, Hama, Homs, Damascus and Bosra remained

*Literally 'overseas', denoting the Latin kingdoms.

independent throughout, as did Baalbek and the Beqa'a Valley, which were subject to the Amirate of Damascus. Syria and the rest of the Levant were thus divided into a coastal zone of Frankish occupation and a large Muslim hinterland, the latter looming ominously and permanently hostile although at times partially co-operative with the invaders.

The Franks were not only territorially confined but also numerically restricted. Of the original 150,000 Crusaders who had responded to the call of Pope Urban and taken up the cross only an estimated 40,000 were present at the siege of Jerusalem. Some had settled in Antioch and Edessa, others had succumbed to disease or died in battle. Numbers were further depleted once the goal of the First Crusade had been attained in taking Jerusalem, since many Crusaders considered themselves absolved of their oath to liberate the Holy Places and now returned home to their families. According to Runciman, the combined 'knightly' population of the Kingdom of Jerusalem never exceeded a thousand knights and barons in permanent residence. Tripoli contained approximately two hundred noble Frankish families. There would have been even fewer had not the march to Jerusalem been almost unopposed as a result of the disunity between the Saljuqs in northern Syria and the Fatimids in the south. The establishment of the Crusader states thus posed the victors with the immediate problem of how such a tiny minority might hold the territory it had so easily won.

Chronic lack of manpower remained a problem throughout the entire period of Frankish occupation. The response to the situation was the construction of a string of mighty fortifications to protect the ports, and of imposing castles in the coastal hills to act both as offensive bridge-heads against the interior and as defensive bastions in times of trouble. Only behind solid masonry could the Crusaders feel relatively secure and enjoy a sense of permanence and home. The castles are their major monuments; it has been argued that they are the only enduring achievement of the Crusades. Without such eloquent and tangible testimony it is conceivable that the Crusades would no longer loom so large in the collective memory. To Syrians they still serve as reminders of the aggression and domination of foreign powers.

Yet, whatever thoughts they might stir in the minds of onlookers and whatever strategic calculations drove those twelfth and thirteenth-century Franks in a strange land to such heights of architectural expression, the remains of their monuments and fortifications appear entirely spontaneous and in harmony with the natural environment. Fedden's description in *Crusader Castles* hits the mark:

'It seems as though these men in carapace of mail produced in the very business of living, like coral insects, cell on cell of stone.' A visit to a number of these Crusader strongholds reveals as much of the reality of life in Outremer as can be gleaned from the writings of historians and chroniclers. The castles are scattered throughout the Near East from Turkey to Jordan but some of the finest examples of the art are to be found in Syria in the ruins of Sahyun, Marqab, Tortosa, Safita and the legendary Krak des Chevaliers.

Sahyun, an advance guard for Latakia and Antioch, sits upon the spur of a mountain in a rugged terrain of jagged rock and scrub trees. Built on the site of an earlier Byzantine fortress, the castle's use of the natural environment for its defence is truly spectacular. The triangular-shaped fortifications are protected on two sides by the steep incline of the mountain itself but the third side has been made secure by the hewing through the solid rock of an immense channel measuring 130 metres long by 20 metres wide and 25 metres deep. The physical toil expended on cutting and removing 65,000 cubic metres of hard stone must have been an undertaking of Pharaonic proportions. A solitary pinnacle of rock has been left standing in order to provide a support for the drawbridge which would otherwise have been unable to span the enormous gap. Historians of military architecture describe the rock channel of Sahyun as an extreme development of the Byzantine fosse but the effect of the work appears so impressively unique as to be without antecedents. Sahyun is also noted for its physical size. Its walls contain an enclosure of more than five hectares which ranks it among the largest of the Crusader castles.

The original Byzantine castle was taken over by the Franks at the beginning of the twelfth century and probably assumed its present aspect around 1120. It was taken by Salah al-Din in 1188, a year after his victory at Hittin, and was never recaptured. Today it has been renamed in his honour as Saladin's castle. Although the Muslim masters added a minaret, a bath and some residential buildings, the essential shape of the castle remained unchanged and as such it is a fine authentic specimen of early Crusader architecture.

Marqab was taken into possession by the Hospitallers in 1186. It became an enormous military bastion usually stocked with enough food to withstand a five-year siege. The strictly defensive aspect of the castle is beautified at Marqab by the chapel whose windows would be at home in a church of thirteenth-century northern France. Yet it is for defence that Marqab is most noted. Its concentric fortifications show the significant shift from the offensive to the defensive as the tide turned in favour of the Muslims, forcing the Crusaders to employ every possible device to secure themselves against attack. The forbidding black basalt of the castle adds a note of gloom and doom to the seeming impregnability of Marqab. Such was its strength as an outpost of the County of Tripoli that Salah al-Din passed it by after the battle of Hittin. In 1270 Sultan Baibars twice failed to take it by assault; the honour was left to his son Qalawun who, in 1285, forced the occupants to surrender after he had undermined the very foundations of the circular tower-keep. It was one of the last of the Frankish strongholds to fall.

Of the coastal fortifications, those at Tortosa (modern Tartus) built by the Knights Templar in the second half of the twelfth century proved to be the most effective. Salah al-Din managed to capture the town in 1188 but failed to take the castle itself where the Templars had taken refuge. Little remains today of the castle of Tortosa except isolated parts, which have been integrated into the growing city. Apartment balconies festooned with washing now decorate the west wall of the stronghold facing the sea. But if present-day development has taken over the castle that successfully withstood every siege attempt, then the Cathedral of Our Lady has miraculously come through unscathed to display intact the fair interior of a fine French church that would stand proudly next to the best examples in Burgundy and Provence. Now serving as a museum, the Cathedral of Tortosa, through its inspired and graceful proportions, reminds us of the original religious motivation behind the First Crusade and of the non-military aspects of life in Outremer. It was from Tortosa that the last of the Crusaders set sail in 1291 for the tiny offshore island of Arwad, where they held out for another eleven years before abandoning Syrian soil forever for exile in Cyprus.

Within sight of Tortosa, but high up in the coastal hills, stands the isolated keep of Safita, the township having long since invaded the outer defences and constructed houses right up to the front door. Chastel Blanc, as the fortification is also known, was built by the Templars and reveals the same religious devotion as witnessed by the Cathedral of Tortosa. Within the keep, and indeed occupying the entire ground floor and two thirds of the total structure, stands not a banqueting hall but a chapel. Chastel Blanc can be seen as the quintessence of Crusader life with its self-contained combination of fortified chapel, audience chamber and underground cistern. From the battlements the Templars of Safita could relay signals to their colleagues-at-arms, the Hospitallers, who resided at the most imposing castle of all, the redoubtable Krak des Chevaliers.

The word 'krak' is thought to derive from the Arabic name Hosn al-Akrad or Castle of the Kurds, with *akrad* being corrupted to *krat* and eventually *krak*. In any event the original 'Castle of the K[urds was the earliest] structure commanding the passage through the hills between the sea and the interior known as the Homs Gap, was one of the stopping-places during the march of the First Crusade on Jerusalem. The words of T.E. Lawrence figure in the descriptions of all commentators: he described it as 'perhaps the best preserved and most wholly admirable castle in the world.' From the Muslim point of view the aesthetic qualities of Krak were overshadowed by the military threat that it posed. Only a day's march from the city of Homs, the Frankish stronghold was in the words of the historian Ibn al-Athir, 'a bone stuck in the very throat of the Muslims'. At the height of its power, at the beginning of the thirteenth century, a garrison of two thousand knights was stationed within its walls, a force capable of launching surprise attacks and quickly withdrawing behind the safety of its concentric fortifications. Salah al-Din marched on Krak after the battle of Hittin but, seeing its strength, marched away again.

Despite the perfection of its defences Krak could not stand for ever. As the Frankish territories receded in the second half of the thirteenth century it became less an offensive bastion and more like a beleaguered outpost. The cost of the upkeep was immense, and manpower was no longer so readily available. There is a poignant letter from Hughes Revel, Grand Master of the Hospitallers, written in 1268 which lists the many difficulties facing the defenders. Three years later the moment of truth arrived, as Sultan Baibars laid siege to the castle. Although it is thought that Baibars resorted to a forged letter, supposedly from the Grand Commander at Tripoli instructing the garrison to surrender, there is no doubt that the outer walls had been penetrated and that the knights had withdrawn to the innermost refuge of the citadel area.

The excellent state of preservation of Krak des Chevaliers today is, as an appropriate gesture to its original builders, due to the work of French restoration specialists. Some 660 years after the fall of the castle a team under the auspices of the 'Académie des Inscriptions et Belles-Lettres' was sent to supervise the clearance and repair of their ancestors' stronghold. In the meantime a village of 530 inhabitants together with their flocks of sheep had installed themselves within the fortifications, taking over substantial amounts of the original mas-onry for the construction of their homes. The work lasted nine years and has restored Krak to its previous splendour. The towers, battlements, stables, the chapel, the Lodge of the Grand Master all stand ready as if for the ghosts of the Knights Hospitaller to return. As Fedden noted in *Crusader Castles*, the silence of Krak is hardly natural: 'The   hat stood upon the north wall should be grinding corn; in the huge   mber ... troops should be quartered; the cry of the watch should echo along the battlements, and in the halls and passages the clank of mailed knights; the guardroom should be noisy with medieval French, and from the chapel should come the chant of the Latin mass. Instead there are only the shadows of the kestrels cruising above, and the sun-scorched stones.'

The popular picture of life in a Crusader castle which fills the pages of both Christian and Muslim chroniclers, is of dramatic sieges. Yet for years on end there would be no military activity to break the routine of the daily round. Part of the architectural achievement, the attention to detail and the ingenious systems of defence, can possibly be ascribed to the fact that the occupying knights had time on their hands. Building new fortifications and improving others must have been a tremendous release of energy for the hundreds, some-times thousands of men cooped up in barrack-like conditions. Indeed, the conditions imposed by the long-term garrisoning of the castles were such that special institutions evolved to fulfil the task. The military orders of fighting monks, the Templars and the Hospitallers – the former recognisable by a red cross on a white background and the latter by a white cross on black – were ideally suited to the rigours of the monastic life. Their vow of celibacy, their dedication to the cross and the strength of their organisations' resources gave them the staying power to remain as islands of resistance long after other conventional forces had been defeated and driven out.

Military discipline was, however, not the only factor involved, for the castles depended to a great extent on the co-operation of the neighbouring villages and agricultural areas to supply them with food and materials. Furthermore, the authority exercised by a strong and equitable castle administration actually encouraged the development of farming in the area under its control. The peasantry had no feudal obligations other than tax payments, mainly in crops, and the bulk of the dues were paid by the community as a whole so that the Frankish master was more akin to a rentier than to a feudal lord. There was a marked contrast between the austerity of castle life and the luxury of the coastal towns where merchant communities from Pisa, Venice, Genoa and Amalfi amassed huge fortunes in trade. The siege-mentality which long periods of confinement induced must have made the Templars and Hospitallers wonder at times whether they were the guardians of the Holy Land or merely prisoners within the walls of their own castles.

It would be a mistake to regard the Franks as the only builders of castles at the time. On the Muslim side too this was the age of castles and fortified strongholds, and the skills of military architects in the unconquered territories reached equally great heights. The Citadel of Aleppo is to the Muslims what the Krak des Chevaliers is to the Crusaders. Situated on a vast mound in the middle of the city, the Citadel of Aleppo has been a military stronghold for thousands of years, going back to the ancient kingdom of Yamhad in the second millennium and probably even further. However, it was during the time of the Crusades that it acquired its present aspect. Under the rule of the Ayyubid Sultan al-Zahir Ghazi, a son of Salah al-Din, the Citadel acquired its monumental gate, the deep moat and the paved slope of the glacis as protection against mines. The mosque and palace within the walls have survived to this day in spite of the ravages of the Mongols led by Hulagu in 1260 and Tamerlane in 1400. In both instances the necessary repair work was carried out by the Mamluks: the two external towers and the second storey of the main gate are fine examples of Mamluk workmanship.

Max van Berchem called the Citadel of Aleppo 'one of the most remarkable productions of Arab military construction', and Ibn Battuta, quoting another Arab chronicler, claimed that it was so high that the stars in the firmament surrounded it like a heavenly belt. Nur al-Din was the founder of a mosque built on the spot where, according to legend, Abraham used to milk his cow. The decoration of this fortification is as impressive as the legends surrounding it: sculptures of lions, dragons and serpents on the magnificent archways appear to serve as evil charms whose magic power would see off any intruder that managed to penetrate the outer shell of this immaculate stronghold.

Damascus also acquired stronger defences during the Crusades and its famous Citadel is one of the best conserved of the large Muslim fortresses. Both Nur al-Din and Salah al-Din made improvements to it but the present building was constructed at the beginning of the thirteenth century. It was in the earlier version of the Citadel of Damascus that Salah al-Din died in 1193, before his brother al-Malik al-Adil had the outer wall reconstructed with the addition of thirteen rectangular towers. After long years of neglect and service as both prison and army barracks the Citadel of Damascus is now being renovated and made accessible.

Probably the most curious fortification in Syria is the Arab castle at Bosra, which was built during the first half of the thirteenth century. Nine rectangular towers and a moat crossed by a solitary bridge give no indication that within – and in a state of perfect preservation – is the original Roman theatre which goes back nine centuries earlier. Another Muslim castle is located at Masyaf, mid-way between Hama and Tartus. This became one of the principal bases of the sinister organisation known as the Assassins. This secretive group had a command structure strangely akin to that of the Templars and Hospitallers, with a Grand Master known familiarly as 'The Old Man of the Mountain'. From the castle at Masyaf the Assassins would go forth on their deadly missions, ready to murder Christians and Muslims alike; more often than not they were in alliance with the Franks. The word 'assassin' has come to us from the name of this group of ritualistic killers who acted as much out of political as religious motives and who were a force to be feared by both sides during the Crusades.

The nearest equivalent on the Muslim side to the classic Crusader castle is the ruined but splendid stronghold at Sheizar, perched on a rocky eminence that forms a gorge on the Orontes. With a commanding view of the river the castle stood as a defensive bulwark against both Franks and the Assassins of nearby Masyaf. Sheizar is interesting both for the independent role it played as a centre of Muslim resistance and for the famous son of its ancestral family, Usama ibn Munqidh, whose chronicles of the period permit unique insights into the complexities of the relations between Muslims and Crusaders. His is one of the most interesting accounts of the Syrian Arabs living during the Crusades, and his long life from 1095 to 1188 spans most of the momentous events of the twelfth century.

Much of Usama's account is concerned with warfare. He describes his first experience of armed combat – albeit as a spectator – at the age of fifteen, and later how he slays his first Frankish knight. For the most part he tells of minor skirmishes, which have otherwise gone unrecorded as being peripheral to the main thrust of the Crusades. More interesting are the periods of cease-fire when Usama travels extensively throughout Frankish-occupied territory and records his experiences and personal reflections. He visits Acre and ransoms some Muslim slaves; in Jerusalem he takes a legal matter to King Fulk and is impressed at how the king refers the litigation to a group of knights whose judgement is accepted as binding. One day Usama receives a letter from Tancred, Prince of Antioch, recommending to his care a Christian pilgrim; in Nablus, while staying in a house which served as an inn for Muslim travellers, he has occasion to wonder at the strange lack of fidelity and honour among Christian couples; he visits a community of ascetics and then of Sufis and is impressed by the piety of the men of each religion.

During these lulls in the fighting he appears to enjoy excellent relations with at least some of the Franks, in particular those who had become used to the ways of the Orient. He observes: 'There are some Franks who have settled in our land and taken to living like Muslims. They are better than those who have just arrived from their homelands.' Usama's famous encounter at the al-Aqsa mosque in Jerusalem with one of those newly arrived from Europe underlines the cultural differences among the Franks:

> 'This is an example of Frankish barbarism, God damn them! When I was in Jerusalem I used to go to the Masjid al-Aqsa, beside which is a small oratory which the Franks have made into a church. Whenever I went into the mosque, which was in the hands of the Templars who were friends of mine, they would put the little oratory at my disposal, so that I could say my prayers there. One day I had gone in, said the "Allah akbar" and risen to begin my prayers, when a Frank threw himself on me from behind, lifted me up and turned me so that I was facing east. "That is the way to pray!" he said. Some Templars at once intervened, seized the man and took him out of my way, while I resumed my prayer. But the moment they stopped watching him he seized me again and forced me to face east, repeating that this was the way to pray. Again the Templars intervened and took him away. They apologised to me and said: "He is a foreigner who has just arrived today from his homeland in the north, and he has never seen anyone pray facing any other direction than east." "I have finished my prayers," I said, and left, stupefied by the fanatic who had been so perturbed and upset to see someone praying facing the "qibla" *!'

Yet all these anecdotal observations are punctuated by scenes of gory fighting in which Usama often played a leading role. His final judgement on the Franks is that they are no better than the wild beasts, although he does concede that they possess great valour and intelligence. The final part of Usama's autobiography is the poignant lament of an octogenarian faced with the daily burden of old age and the imminent prospect of death. At one time he likens his existence to that of a camel that has been constantly harried about in the desert and at another he complains that he is reduced to passing his days reclined upon a sofa and is obliged by reason of his declining strength to pray in seated position. He who

*The wall of the mosque which is oriented towards Mecca.

had so many close encounters with death is now kept waiting for deliverance. Usama eventually expired at the age of ninety-three.

Usama fought alongside Salah al-Din on many occasions and the two men shared the same humane intelligence. At the heart of the legend surrounding Salah al-Din lies his humanity, but this was usually coupled to a keen understanding of human behaviour. After recapturing Jerusalem not only did he allow the vanquished to ransom their lives but he did not prevent the King of Jerusalem departing with vast quantities of church treasure. Imad al-Din relays the words of Salah al-Din to justify what appeared to others as soft treatment: 'If we interpret the treaty to their disadvantage they will accuse us of breaking faith and of being ignorant of the true essence of the thing. I prefer to make them obey the letter of the treaty, so that they are then unable to accuse the Believers of breaking their word, but will tell others of the benefits we have bestowed upon them.' Certainly, Salah al-Din's scrupulous honesty won him great respect from the Franks but in the main it was never reciprocated as he would have hoped.

The picture on the Frankish side was not entirely bleak, but it is a mistake to insist too much on the arts of peace promoted by the Franks and to beguile oneself into seeing only the settlement process which Paul Deschamps described as a 'pénétration pacifique'. It is always necessary to recall the bloody overture to the Crusades, the sack of Jerusalem in 1099 perpetrated by the Franks. Ibn al-Athir tells the sorry tale:

> 'In the Masjid al-Aqsa the Franks slaughtered more than 70,000 people, among them a large number of Imams and Muslim scholars, devout and ascetic men who had left their homelands to live lives of pious seclusion in the Holy Place. The Franks stripped the Dome of the Rock ... Refugees from Syria reached Baghdad in Ramadan*. They told the Caliph's ministers a story that wrung their hearts and brought tears to their eyes. On Friday they went to the mosque and begged for help, weeping so that their hearers wept with them as they described the sufferings of the Muslims in that Holy City: the men killed, the women and children taken prisoner, the homes pillaged.'

Runciman, in *A History of the Crusades*, comments on the sack of Jerusalem: 'It

*The Islamic month of fasting.

was this bloodthirsty act of Christian fanaticism that recreated the fanaticism of Islam. When, later, wiser Latins in the East sought to find some basis on which Christian and Moslem could work together, the memory of the massacre stood always in their way.'

There is no escaping the deep contradictions of the Crusades, no way to reconcile the slaughter and the religious purpose that supposedly lay behind them. On the one hand the Crusades were conceived as a divine mission, but never in the sense of missionary activity. It appears that the Crusaders were at best unconcerned with converting the Muslims and more often than not actually prevented it. In contrast to the Muslim conquest of Syria and Palestine in the seventh century, which initially avoided land-ownership, territorial possession was paramount to the Crusaders, who felt what some commentators have termed a 'land-hunger'. Furthermore, there were many conflicting interests and ambitions within their camp: the Templars and the Hospitallers answered directly to the Pope and often displayed a lack of co-operation with the secular authorities in Jerusalem, Tripoli and Antioch, while the profit motives of the Italian merchant communities in the ports took precedence over the Christian cause. Edward of England was shocked to discover that the Venetians and Genoese were doing lucrative business with the Mamluk Sultans as arms suppliers.

Perhaps the basic dilemma of Outremer lay in its confused policies. On the one hand it was waging a Holy War and on the other it was seeking to set up permanent colonies. The Frankish knights first established themselves in Syria and Palestine as a military and religious aristocracy; but the Frankish nobility remained an alien element, did not attempt to assimilate the local population into its ranks and failed to develop any cultural common identity, not even with the local Christians. Instead, they withdrew behind stout walls of racial and doctrinal exclusivity. It was perhaps the greatest single blunder of the Crusaders that they treated the Christians of the East and Byzantium as the enemies of the Latin faith. On this point the verdict of history is straightforward: 'The Crusades were launched to save Eastern Christendom from the Moslems. When they ended the whole of Eastern Christendom was under Moslem rule... Seen in the perspective of history the whole crusading movement was a vast fiasco.' *

Outremer, in geopolitical terms, remained an artificial entity, largely depen-

*Runciman, *A History of the Crusades.*

dent on foreign aid and manpower. The surprising point is not that it did not last but that it managed to hold out for so long. In terms of cultural progress the Franks took back to Europe some skills and oriental luxuries, but the Muslims learned little from the Franks, except in the science of military architecture. Men like Usama ibn Munqidh, who displayed an interest and respect for the culture of the other side, were too few to count for much in the face of the entrenched opinions of the majority; and the conclusion of Runciman's final volume of *A History of the Crusades*, although harsh, is difficult to refute: 'In the long sequence of interaction and fusion between Orient and Occident ... the Crusades were a tragic and destructive episode ... There was so much courage and so little honour, so much devotion and so little understanding. High ideals were besmirched by cruelty and greed, enterprise and endurance by a blind and narrow self-righteousness; and the Holy War itself was nothing more than a long act of intolerance in the name of God, which is a sin against the Holy Ghost.'

CHAPTER SIX

Damascus
and Aleppo

Most archaeological sites in Syria represent several distinct periods of civilisation but Damascus and Aleppo run through the entire course of Syrian history and much of its prehistory as well. In contrast to the deserted sites such as Palmyra, Mari, and the Dead Cities, in Damascus and Aleppo the old and the ancient are intermingled with the new in a way that is often difficult to unravel. Roman, Byzantine, Umayyad, Ayyubid, Mamluk and Ottoman do not appear as neat layers in a scientifically excavated tell but are hopelessly jumbled on the surface. In fact, due to the density of present occupation, it has not been possible to conduct the extensive excavations necessary to reconstruct the exact development of these towns which are both advanced as being the oldest continuously inhabited cities in the world.

Damascus can claim the valuable support of Islamic legend as the Garden of Eden. It was also in Damascus that the birthplace of Abraham is said to be situated, and there is a grotto in Mount Kassioun which overlooks the city where Cain is thought to have concealed the body of his brother Abel. According to the twelfth-century Arab traveller, Ibn Jubayr, 'The blood reaches from about half-way up the mountain to the cave, and God has preserved red traces of it on the stones . . .' Isolated patches of red rock occur in the vicinity to remind us of this original fratricide. A more pleasant association is based on the Quranic verse (*XXIII, 50*), 'We made the son of Mary and his mother a sign to mankind and gave them a shelter on a peaceful hill-side watered by a fresh spring'. There was a popular Damascene tradition which made the river Barada the site mentioned in the Quran.

By far the most potent of all the legends attached to Damascus is that which concerns the Prophet Mohammed himself. It is said that Mohammed stopped when he saw the green splendour of the Damascus oasis known as al-Ghouta and turned back towards Mecca for fear that to enter paradise in this world might endanger his chances of paradise in the world hereafter. The village of Qadem to the south of Damascus is named after the footprint of the Prophet and the event is commemorated in the local mosque.

Visions of the Damascus oasis as an earthly paradise have been nurtured by the original physical beauty of the site. The river Barada and the spring known as Ain al-Fijah come together in the mountains of the Anti-Lebanon and flood down towards the desert to create a patch of natural paradise on the fringe of the desert. The dramatic contrast between the oasis and the wasteland around gives rise to the curious definition of 'arid subtropical' in the language of climatology. Most writers describe the phenomenal beauty of the setting with unbridled passion and intensity. Kinglake's romantic vision succeeds in conveying the total dependence of Damascus on the waters of the Barada: 'As a man falls flat face forward on the brook, that he may drink and drink again; so Damascus, thirsting for ever, lies down with her lips to the stream, and clings to its rushing waters.' Without a river there would have been no city on the fringe of the Syrian desert.

It is hardly surprising that such a place attracted human settlement from the earliest beginnings of organised communities. Excavations at Ramad have revealed evidence of permanent occupation at the very end of the seventh millennium BC and archaeological investigation in the vicinity of Damascus gives the city a span of at least 8000 and as much as 10,000 years. The city properly enters the realm of history in the middle of the second millennium BC as the centre of an Aramaean kingdom, known as Aram, but there are also some references to the place in the third millennium BC in the Ebla tablets. The Aramaean presence is attested also by the discovery of a basalt orthostat depicting a sphinx, excavated in the north-east corner of the Umayyad mosque, and it is thought that a temple of the period lies beneath. References to the events at the beginning of the first millennium BC in the Old Testament document the struggle over Aram between the Israelites in the west and the Assyrians in the east. In 732 BC Aram fell to the Assyrian Tiglathpileser III and remained subordinate to the Babylonians and then to the Persians in the pre-Hellenistic period.

Sadly, nothing remains visible of the Aramaean settlement but it is known that it was they who first established the water distribution system of Damascus by constructing canals and tunnels, collectively known as *qanawat*, which ensured that maximum use was made of the river Barada before its waters emptied out into brackish lakes on the desert verge. This same network, later improved by the Romans and the Umayyads, still forms the basis of the water system of Damascus in the twentieth century. By skilful hydraulic engineering the Barada is not one but seven rivers, which reach every part of the old city and provide as a bonus a much appreciated natural air-conditioning. It is a measure of the longevity and continuity of life in Damascus that the water which bubbles up so delightfully in many a fountain set in a private courtyard comes through channels first laid some three thousand years ago.

With the passing of the Aramaeans the city of Aram eventually re-emerged as Dimashq ash-Sham, known according to the English convention as Damascus. The name still causes much confusion to experts in philology and semantics. Possible origins of the name have been linked both to biblical and Greek legend and there are suggestions that the word in Aramaic designated 'city of abundant water' or 'oasis'. Those seeking an Arabic root are left with a word that means 'speedy' or 'fleet of foot', when applied to a camel. Damascus, however obscure its origins, is the name which became permanently affixed to the place.*

During the time of the Seleucids the city was of minor importance in relation to the new Hellenistic foundations of Apamea, Laodicea and Antioch. For a while during the ensuing Roman period it was held by the Nabataean kings of Petra. Its re-emergence into the limelight of history began with the occupation by the Romans in 64 BC and subsequent incorporation into the strategic Near Eastern league of ten cities known as the Decapolis. Damascus became a metropolis at the beginning of the second century AD and in 222 it was upgraded to a *colonia* by the Emperor Septimius Severus, who had married the Syrian Julia Domna. The Pax Romana provided security for commerce across the desert and gave Damascus in particular and Syria in general an era of prosperity and settled government.

This was the first great moment for Damascus as a caravan city. Nature had provided the Barada oasis but the trade routes of the first centuries AD endowed Damascus with a strategic location which was to lay the foundations of the city's wealth. The incense routes from the lands of southern Arabia and the silk traffic from China all converged on Damascus, making it one of the great trade counters of the period. The Roman demand for eastern luxuries was satisfied

*Syrians refer to the city simply as ash-Sham.

by the caravans which arrived via Palmyra and the incense was carried from the south via the Nabataean city of Petra. The lucrative commerce in goods was supplemented by the skill of the city's artisans, who worked the silk and gold into fine brocades and forged blades of steel which have made the name Damascus famous throughout the world.

Although little remains of the architecture of the Romans, the building activity and town planning of this time have had a lasting – indeed indelible – effect on the subsequent development and thus the present aspect of the old city. The Romans brought together the adjacent Greek and Aramaean foundations and incorporated them into a new layout measuring approximately 1500 by 750 metres, enclosed within a city wall pierced by seven gates. Only the eastern gate, Bab Sharqi, remains from the Roman period, but the walls, although rebuilt more than once in the Islamic period, still follow the original course laid out by the Romans. During the third century AD, construction started on the Temple of Jupiter. This temple, following the pattern of the temples to Baal in Palmyra and Baalbek, consisted of a vast courtyard, of which the walls are preserved around the present Umayyad Mosque. This sacred area was set within an outer precinct so that the total space occupied a site measuring 315 by 270 metres. The monumental entrance on the western side can still be identified by the group of pillars at the inner end of the main suq of Damascus, the Hamidiye. Of the actual shrine to Jupiter and indeed of the cathedral which followed it, nothing remains.

Although Roman Damascus lies mostly at depths of up to five metres below the modern city and little can be seen at street level, a glance into the cellars of many houses reveals parts of classical columns supporting foundations. The house of Ananias, which now serves as an underground chapel, is at the level of Damascus in the days of St Paul just prior to the Roman occupation. Aerial photography and cartography has revealed how much of the Roman street plan has imposed its pattern on the subsequent Islamic city map. Most obviously the Street called Straight follows the exact course of the old *via recta*, extending for about 1.5 kilometres from the Bab Sharqi. Although in places it is reduced to as little as one quarter of its original twenty-six metres width, as a result of extensions to the suqs, it is still the main thoroughfare of the old city. The triumphal arch, located close to the mid-point of the street, is not in its correct position but was excavated nearby. It serves, however, to remind those passing by of the Roman origin of the street. Close scrutiny of the street plan of Damascus shows quite clearly that the city was once divided into regular blocks measuring 100 by 45 metres, and from the present alignment of the houses it is just possible to detect the outline of what was once the theatre, the palace and the forum.

During the ensuing Christian era it would appear that the outward aspect of Damascus did not suffer much alteration. It is unclear whether the Temple of Jupiter served to house the Cathedral of St John the Baptist, whose head is supposed to lie buried in the Umayyad Mosque. The only possible clue to the physical appearance of Damascus under Byzantium is to be sought in the famous mosaics of the Umayyad Mosque known as the Barada panel. In as far as this represents the vicinity of Damascus in the seventh century AD the stylised landscape of houses, palaces, roads, bridges and the river itself testifies only to the Byzantine style of the architecture and no clue is given to the size and shape of the city it might portray. In any case, the caliphate of the Umayyads which made Damascus the centre of the expanding Arab empire in 661 would remodel the main features of the city.

The Great Mosque of the Umayyads (see Chapter Four) was the most spectacular and is the only surviving structure of this period*. The green-domed palace of Muawiya has disappeared without trace. Yet the new canal cut by Yezid still functions and bears the name of the caliph himself. The river system bequeathed by the Aramaeans and the Romans was further extended so that fresh water flowed to the fountains of houses throughout the city. During the reign of Walid, Damascus reached its peak as the centre of the first Arab-Islamic empire which extended from the Far East to the Atlantic Ocean. Yet the Umayyad glory was short-lived and after 750 the Abbasids in Baghdad consistently promoted their city on the Tigris at the expense of Damascus. The Syrian capital sank into a long period of economic and social stagnation which reflected the radically changed political circumstances. The measure of the decline of Damascus can be gauged from the fact that not one building exists to mark the 450 years between the Great Mosque of the Umayyads and the Hospital of Nur al-Din in 1154. Nevertheless the Abbasid caliphs were drawn to Damascus, according to Ibn Asakir, for its clean air and beautiful countryside, and al-Muhallabi al-Bahnassi reported in the tenth century that no place on earth possessed so many flowers and trees: 'The Valley of Violets four miles in length and traversed by the Barada is entirely covered by a forest of cyprus trees and the sun's rays rarely touch the ground.' This natural paradise became in the eleventh century the scene of a bitter struggle between the Fatimids and the

---

*In 1984 the outer walls of the Umayyad Mosque were cleared of intrusive constructions.

Saljuqs, which resulted in the latter assuming control of the city in 1076.

The first half of the twelfth century saw three successive attacks on Damascus by the Crusaders before Nur al-Din succeeded in taking the city in 1154 and uniting Syria against the Franks. Nur al-Din not only played a crucial role in the revival of the Muslim cause but he inaugurated a period of reconstruction and development for the city. The hospital and medical school he founded in the very year he wrested control of Damascus from the Saljuqs still stands as a fitting memorial to his respect for men of science; at the time it was the most advanced medical institution in the world. His funerary *madrasa* or college, known as al-Nuriya, described by Ibn Jubayr as one of the best schools in the world, introduced the notion of a mausoleum serving as the foundation of a school of Quranic learning. This was but one of many *madrasas* founded by Nur al-Din in order to propagate Sunnite at the expense of Shi'ite doctrine. Both the college, the Madrasa al-Nuriya, and the hospital, Bimaristan Nur al-Din, have survived to this day, and the memory of their founder is held in great reverence. Nur al-Din's rule in Damascus (1154–74), although set against the menacing background of the Crusades, was marked by other public works such as baths which belie the military mood of the times. However, defence was not over-looked: Nur al-Din renovated the city walls and made major improvements to the Citadel. In all his undertakings he was emulated by his more illustrious successor and the founder of Ayyubid rule, Salah al-Din.

Under Salah al-Din and the Ayyubids Damascus continued to prosper. The suburb of Salihiye, peopled by refugees from Jerusalem, was built *extra muros* at the foot of Mount Kassioun. The Citadel was rebuilt and further improve-ments made to the defences of the city. The Citadel became not only a last refuge for a besieged garrison but also provided quarters for the sultan as well as storage for provisions and ammunition. The mint and a prison were also included within its walls. And it was here, in a small room in the Citadel of Damascus, that Salah al-Din passed away in 1193.

The Damascus of Salah al-Din is brilliantly evoked by the account of the Arab traveller Ibn Jubayr, who spent several months in the city in 1184. He writes: 'Damascus is the paradise of the Orient and dawning place of her gracious and resplendent beauty . . . The gardens encircle it like the halo round the moon and contain it as it were the calyx of a flower. To the east, its green Ghoutah stretches as far as the eye can see, and wherever you look on its four sides its ripe fruits hold the gaze.' As for the inside of the city, Ibn Jubayr relates: '. . . its streets were narrow and dark, and its houses were made of mud and reeds, arranged in three storeys one over the other so that fire speedily took hold of them. Damascus contained as many as three cities, for it was the most populous in the world. Its beauty was all outside, not in. The markets of Damascus were the finest in the world and the best arranged, and the most handsomely constructed.' There is also an ecstatic description of the Umayyad Mosque, a reference to some twenty colleges in the city, a rhapsodic portrait of the view from Mount Kassioun and an account of the Sultan playing polo on the playing fields next to the Citadel 'so green as to seem to be rolls of silk brocade'.

In Ibn Jubayr's diary of his stay in Damascus there is a marked contrast between the open spaces outside and the narrow and dark streets within. As external security improved so suburbs developed and Salihiye evolved in the thirteenth and fourteenth centuries as a self-contained township outside the city walls. Salah al-Din's Ayyubid successors did not last long and little remains in Damascus to mark their passing except his mausoleum and that of his brother al-Adil, known as the Madrasa Adiliya. Salihiye's growing importance is marked by the Hanabila Mosque and the Bimaristan al-Qaymari, both con-structed in the thirteenth century.

In 1260 Damascus suffered its first bitter experience of assault by the Mongols under Hulagu, a grandson of Ghengiz Khan. Having left a trail of butchery from Baghdad to Aleppo the Mongols took Damascus, tearing down the Citadel and burning the palace of the Ayyubid princes. Further devastation was only avoided by the arrival of the Mamluk Sultan Qutuz who defeated the Mongols at Ain Jalut (Goliath Spring). Henceforth Damascus was governed by the Mamluks and a new stimulus was given to the development of the city.

Surprisingly for a dynasty which sprang from a line of tough Circassian slaves, the Mamluks devoted much energy to decorative refinement and were lovers of good building. The Madrasa Zahiriya, the mausoleum-cum-college of Sultan Baibars built in 1278, is one of several imposing Mamluk monuments to have survived through the ages. Other examples of fourteenth-century Mamluk foundations are the Tinkiz Mosque and the al-Aqsab. The latter was originally built in 1321 but had to be rebuilt in 1408 following the most disastrous visi-tation by the Mongols that Damascus was to endure.

In 1400 Timur, or Tamerlane, descended on the glittering world of Mamluk Damascus. At the time the city was considered by some European travellers to be superior to Paris and Florence. Ibn Battuta, the great Arab travel writer of the fourteenth century, noted in 1326 a frenzy of building activity: 'The people of Damascus vie with one another in building mosques, religious houses, colleges and mausolea'. At the time the city was the centre of skilled artisans and of the largest and most respected pilgrimage to Mecca, and in fact Ibn Battuta left the city with one of the pilgrim caravans. Elsewhere he comments: 'Damascus surpasses all other cities in beauty and no description, however full, can do justice to its charms'. The Mongol hordes of Timur appear to have meted out cruelty and devastation to Damascus almost as a measured response to the beauty and refinement of the place. The city of silk, cotton, glassware, jewels, porcelain, pottery, metalwork, leather, paper, soap, spices, perfumes, rose-water, silver, gold and all manner of fruit, flowers and delicacies found itself at the mercy of Timur. Ibn Taghri-Birdi's account of the fate of Damascus is a chilling tale of the bestiality of the Mongols:

> '... Timur declared his amnesty null and void, divided the harahs (quarters) of the city amongst his amirs, who entered it with their courtiers, collected more money, inflicted more punishment on the people, using all brutal means, including burning people alive and hanging others by their heads from the battlements of the walls. They then proceeded to abduct women and younger boys, abusing them publicly... The people of Damascus never experienced anything like that in their long history.
>
> When the amirs had satisfied their desires, they left the city. Then Timur gave Damascus to his men, who repeated the same things with more savagery and brutality. They took with them all males of over five years, and then they set fire to the city, which lasted for three days and nights.
>
> Thus Timur, who had laid siege to the city for eighty days, departed northward, having destroyed the noble Damascus walls, houses, qaysariyas (public buildings), baths, and, above all, mosques. The city was in ruins inhabited only by children.'

How long it took Damascus to recover – if indeed it recovered completely – is difficult to assess. The capture of all the skilled craftsmen and their removal to Samarkand to embellish the Mongol capital was a severe blow. Bertrand de la Brocquière, visiting Damascus in the middle of the fifteenth century, reported: 'Vestiges of this disaster now remain; and toward the gate of St Paul there is a whole quarter that has never been rebuilt.' Yet at the same time we learn from the same writer: 'Damascus may contain, as I have heard, one hundred thousand souls. The town is rich, commercial, and, after Cairo, the most consider-able of all in the possession of the sultan.'

After the Mongol disaster, the rule of the Mamluks resumed and a measure of stability returned, notably during the reign of Qait-bay (1468–95). In spite of regular outbreaks of plague, fifteenth-century Damascus appears to have re-gained much of its former prosperity. Mamluk building was, however, no longer on the scale of the fourteenth century and architectural historians point to a trend towards ornamentation for its own sake. The Mamluk period in Damascus ended with the construction between 1509 and 1515 of the Madrasa Sibaiya. In 1516 the Ottoman Turks defeated the Mamluks, and Selim I assumed the leadership of the Islamic community as the 'Vicar of Allah on Earth'. For the next four hundred years Syria lay under the dominion of the Ottomans.

The development of Damascus during the Ottoman era continued apace. Although enormous taxes were extorted from the citizens, there were in return some impressive public works and remarkable monuments to document the period. Ottoman building showed both a continuation of certain Mamluk traditions as well as a reintroduction of some elements of the old style of Byzantium. Selim I inaugurated this new architectural phase with a mosque and mausoleum around the tomb of the mystic Muhyi al-Din Ibn Arabi in the quarter of Salihiye at the foot of Mount Kassioun. The minaret is reminiscent of the later works of the Mamluks. The next great work of the Ottomans was to bring a new style and harmony to the city and to erect a building which has become a focal point of the modern quarters springing up outside the walls.

The Tekkieh of Suleiman the Magnificent, built in 1554 on the site of the palace of the Mamluk Sultan Baibars, represented a fresh interpretation of the traditional *madrasa* and drew its inspiration from the religious architecture of St Sophia in Constantinople. The series of broad domes and graceful minarets, which resemble the form of pencils, rise against a background of cypress trees to give the city a new skyline. In 1566 a separate, smaller *madrasa* was completed immediately adjacent to the Tekkieh. This was followed in 1571 by the Mosque of Darwish Pasha and in 1586 by the Mosque of Sinan Pasha, which is noted for its minaret clad entirely with green tiles.

Secular buildings make their appearance in the eighteenth century with the construction of the great *khans* or caravanserais to house visiting merchants and their goods. The Khan al-Harir, Khan al-Gumruk and Khan Suleyman Pasha are imposing enough, but the masterpiece of the genre is without doubt the magnificent Khan Asad Pasha which was completed towards the end of the eighteenth century. The French poet Lamartine, visiting Damascus in 1833, likened its enormous dome to that of St Peter's in Rome. The interior of the building consists of a vast courtyard with a fountain, around which are grouped offices and storage facilities. Two upper storeys of individual rooms for the merchants are reached by means of galleries, a design now copied in modern hotels. Decoration is kept to a minimum, in keeping with the business function of the place, but the strength of the columns and arches and the alternating layers of black and white masonry give the Khan Asad Pasha its singular architectural beauty.

Asad Pasha al-Azm, founder of the *khan* which bears his name, was of a prominent Damascene family and one of the most enlightened administrators of Damascus during the Ottoman period. The Azm Palace, the most sumptuous private dwelling in the city, was constructed around 1749 and was such a major undertaking that while work was in progress no craftsmen or labourers could be found for other projects. It is reported that the search for suitable building materials extended as far as Bosra and Dera'a and that parts of the Damascus suq were demolished in order to obtain ancient stone and wooden beams. The Azm Palace is located on the site of the palace of the Mamluk Sultan Tingiz and possibly a princely Umayyad residence once stood on the same spot. Although Asad Pasha was murdered in the bath by orders of the Sublime Porte, the palace he created remained in the possession of his descendants until 1920. The peace and harmony of its courtyards with their fountains and elegant architecture make the Azm Palace a masterpiece of a stately town residence of the eighteenth century. There were other fine mansions constructed during this period, many of which have since disappeared. Notably, the Nassan House has survived as a good example of the decorative techniques and design work of eighteenth-century Damascus. Nor should it be forgotten that there were scores of delightful houses which have remained anonymous.

The presence of the Ottomans in Syria extended into the twentieth century and was only terminated by their defeat in the Great War of 1914–18. Thus, it was during the Ottoman time that Damascus acquired the first instalment of modernisation in terms of urban technology and planning. During the second half of the nineteenth and the opening years of the twentieth century the first modern residential areas outside the old town were constructed, the Suq al-Hamidiye was laid out and wider roads were driven through parts of the old city. The electric tram made its appearance as well as the steam train and the curious station building of the Hijaz railway (1903) stands as one of the last monuments to the four hundred years of Ottoman rule which provide the link between the Middle Ages and the present day. The evolution of modern Damascus, that is since about 1920, bears the familiar hallmark of international urban planning and contemporary architecture and may be considered separately from the specifically Syrian or Damascene cultural heritage to be discerned in the buildings and monuments erected in the course of the preceding centuries.

Although Damascus has consistently been the hub of Syrian national life it has often been eclipsed in terms of commerce and size by the city of Aleppo in the north of the country. The two cities are in a sense the magnetic poles of Syria, each attracting its share of business and political influence. The original site of Damascus was given by nature in the form of the oasis created by the river Barada. In Aleppo, nature was less generous with her gifts and the city's river, the Kowaik, is a meagre stream compared to the rushing torrent of the seven branches of the Barada. The region of Aleppo is compensated by an average rainfall twice that of the Damascus oasis with the result that the city has been able to draw on the agricultural produce of its hinterland.

The actual site of the city might seem arbitrary; it is but one of several hills to emerge from the plateau of northern Syria and does not appear to be an obvious spot for a major settlement, until its strategic importance is taken into consideration. Situated mid-way between the Mediterranean coast and the closest bend in the Euphrates, before the river's course may be retraced north-east towards its source in the Taurus mountains, Aleppo's commercial and military significance becomes apparent. It commands the shortest caravan crossing between east and west, the ideal trade counter for the silk traffic from China as well as the Indian merchandise which arrived by way of the Arabian Gulf and the Euphrates. The advantages of this location have been skilfully and consistently exploited by generations of merchants in Aleppo. It is business acumen rather than natural endowments which have given the city its special character. Although exposed to broadly the same historical forces as Damascus, Aleppo has, as a result of its different geographic situation, responded in its own manner; and the further back one goes in history the more individual appear the destinies of these two cities that are now united within one country.

The history of the city may be dated through epigraphic evidence to the third millennium, when it is mentioned in inscriptions discovered at Ur and Lagash from the time of Sargon of Akkad, and its occupation has been continuous since then. The tablets from the palace of Zimri-Lim at Mari mention Aleppo as the kingdom of Yamhad in the eighteenth century BC. However, the first references to Aleppo as such pre-date the period of Yamhad and use the ancient Amorite root, 'Hal-pa-a-pa' (modern Arabic Halab), of the third millennium BC when the city was part of the Akkadian empire. As for the kingdom of Yamhad in the second millennium BC it is known that it was dominant in the region and had sufficient influence in the power politics of the time to offer succour to Zimri-Lim of Mari and eventually to have him re-installed on his throne. In the immediate context of northern Syria Yamhad was rivalled only by Qatna and Ebla. As has been related (see Chapter One), the city state of Ebla fell under the sway of Yamhad around 1800 BC and both fell to the Hittites some two hundred years later.

Despite challenges from the Mitannians and the Egyptians under Ramses I, the Hittites held sway in Aleppo until the end of the twelfth century BC when their empire was devastated by the 'Sea Peoples'. There followed a Syro-Hittite period when Aleppo was subordinate to an Aramaean kingdom. The Assyrians invaded in their turn and the city's importance remained much diminished in the Babylonian and Persian eras. Its fortunes experienced a considerable boost under the Seleucids when it was known by the ephemeral name of Beroea. Aleppo's pre-Hellenistic roots are thus firmly in Hittite culture, whereas those of Damascus are of Aramaean origin. The tell of Aleppo was probably the site of ancient temples dedicated to a succession of Semitic deities such as Haddad, Ishtar, Shamash, Dagan and Sin.

Hellenistic Beroea profited enormously from the changed political circumstances which made Antioch the capital of the Seleucid realm in Syria. This gave a considerable stimulus to trade, although the subsequent development of Palmyra during the Roman period must have been to the disadvantage of the merchants of Beroea/Aleppo. It would seem that the economic potential of Aleppo was not fully realised until the Islamic period. Little remains of the pre-Islamic city except the layout of certain streets in the suq area which follow the classical pattern. Some elements exist of the Byzantine cathedral built by the Empress Helena which have been incorporated into the new structure of the Madrasa Halawiya. Whatever the importance had been of Byzantine Beroea, the city was thoroughly destroyed in AD 540 by the Persians and it was not to recover until the Islamic era. With the passing of Byzantium, Beroea reverted to its old name of Halab. The Umayyad caliphs, who devoted so much energy to the development of Damascus, had little effect on Aleppo which held almost no administrative significance for them. The Umayyad Mosque of Aleppo was founded, according to Ibn al-Adin, by Suleiman ibn Abd al-Malik in order to rival that built by his brother Walid in Damascus. Although this ambition related to the decoration of the mosque it is clear that it also emulated the layout of the Umayyad Mosque in Damascus. Unfortunately, only the ground plan of the Umayyad Mosque in Aleppo can be detected, due to destruction and re-construction in the twelfth and thirteenth centuries. The oldest remaining part of the mosque as it appears today is the fine, square minaret which dates from 1090–5, and is considered to be one of the best examples of mediaeval Syrian masonry. The outer walls and the pavement of the courtyard are from the time of Zangi and Nur al-Din. The rest is the work of the Mamluks in the fourteenth and fifteenth centuries.

Thus the Umayyad Mosque of Aleppo illustrates the main stages in the city's development in the Islamic period, with the exception, however, of the brilliant Hamdanid dynasty in the tenth century. This was the time of the legendary Sayf al-Dawla (Sword of the State), whose dazzling court and campaigns against the Byzantines were immortalised by the famous bard al-Mutannabbi. Nothing remains of the Aleppo of Sayf al-Dawla, and his fairy-tale palace has disap-peared without a trace. In architectural terms Aleppo's existing heritage really begins with Nur al-Din in the twelfth century.

Although Aleppo's main role was as a bastion to repel the armies of the Crusaders – the city provided Nur al-Din with a military base from which to carry out the re-unification of Syria – much energy was expended on public works of a civilian nature. His successors, Salah al-Din and the Ayyubids, bequeathed Aleppo such fine buildings as the shrine of al-Husain, founded in 1173 and reconstructed in 1200 by Zahir Ghazi, a son of Salah al-Din. Zahir Ghazi's own *madrasa*, the Zahiriya and the adjacent al-Firdous (Paradise), founded by his widow in 1233, belong to the finest creations of the Ayyubid period. Zahir Ghazi's mausoleum-cum-college, built by his son in 1223, stands fittingly oppo-site the Citadel of Aleppo, for the complete rebuilding of its walls, towers and entrance gate was also due to the boundless energies of the son of the great Salah al-Din. Under the Ayyubids extensive canalisation works were carried out and it has been estimated that no less than 194 baths were to be found in thirteenth-century Aleppo. One of the most beautiful founded in this period, the Hammam al-Labbadiye, is located next to the Citadel, although its present aspect is due largely to reconstruction work in the fourteenth century.

The Ayyubid period ended with the first Mongol attack on Aleppo in 1260, when fifty thousand of its citizens were put to the sword. The Mamluks then inaugurated an era of relative stability and great architectural activity. The Citadel was repaired and reinforced and many buildings of merit were constructed in the city, notably the Bimaristan Arghoun, the Saraoui, al-Outrouch and al-Qadi mosques as well as numerous *khans*, baths and mausolea. As in Damascus so in Aleppo the Mamluks promoted a great boom in architecture, the arts and handicrafts. Their efforts to defend Aleppo against the Mongol hordes of Timur in 1400, however, were in vain. For three days Aleppo was given over to plunder and the Citadel was taken by direct assault. Twenty thousand of the citizens were butchered and many of the fine buildings of Nur al-Din and the Ayyubids were destroyed.

In spite of the devastation caused by the Mongols, Aleppo made considerable progress during the twelfth to fifteenth centuries. The city expanded to the north and the west so that the Citadel was no longer a part of the outer defences but an inner refuge in case of emergency. With the transfer of power to the Ottomans in 1516 the strategic location of Aleppo realised its full potential not only as an entrepot for trade between east and west but as a supplier of exotic goods to the new masters in Constantinople. From the sixteenth century Aleppo's commercial fortunes reached unexpected heights. By the end of the eighteenth, Aleppo had become the largest city in Syria with a population of 200,000 and ranked as the third most important in the Ottoman dominions after Constantinople and Cairo. The opulence of the Aleppine merchants attracted fast growing interest among the nations of Europe and diplomatic relations followed in the wake of trade. Consulates were opened in Aleppo by Venice in 1548, France in 1562, England in 1583 and Holland in 1613. The widespread territories of the Ottoman Empire effectively abolished all customs barriers in the Middle East. Although taxes were high there was no impediment to the movement of goods, and most of the goods found their way to the trade counters of Aleppo.

A highly informative account of the city in the eighteenth century under the Ottomans, which is a marvel of objective reporting, is titled *The Natural History of Aleppo*. This is the scientific-sounding title of a two-volume survey which ranges from the intimacies of the harem to a description of the flora and fauna. The work was published in 1794 as the joint effort of the brothers Alexander and Patrick Russell, both doctors in the service of the Levant Company which maintained a factory or trading establishment in Aleppo. Alexander's sojourn in the city was from 1740 to 1753 and that of Patrick from 1750 to 1768. As physicians, both had access to local society which would normally be denied to foreigners and both were scientifically minded in the enlightened tradition of the eighteenth century. Their work is thus of great documentary value. The opening passage of *The Natural History of Aleppo* gives an indication of the style and approach of the brothers Alexander and Patrick:

> 'Aleppo, the present metropolis of Syria, is deemed, in importance, the third city in the Ottoman dominions. In situation, magnitude, population, and opulence, it is much inferior to Constantinople and Cairo; nor can it presume to emulate the courtly splendour of those cities. But in salubrity of air, in the solidity and elegance of its private buildings, as well as the convenience and neatness of its streets, Aleppo may be reckoned superior to both: and though no longer possessed of the same commercial advantages as in former times, it still continues to maintain a share of trade far from inconsiderable.'

The population of Aleppo is given as 235,000, of which 200,000 were Muslims, comprising both Turks and native Aleppines, 30,000 local Christians, 5,000 other Orientals and a tiny expatriate community of Europeans from England, France, Venice, Holland and Tuscany. Most of the European merchants were single and had almost no contact with the people of Aleppo except for business. This was conducted from a series of great *khans* which also provided living quarters. These magnificent premises are one of the lasting glories of Aleppo. Notable among them are the Khan al-Saboun which dates back to the Mamluk era, the Khan al-Gumruk (sixteenth century) and the Khan al-Wazir (seventeenth century). Yet, for their inmates, the beauty of these fine limestone buildings, with their carved window decorations and stately courtyards, must have paled. Their lives were so tightly circumscribed that they were even locked in at night: 'In such a recluse situation, the manner of life, in some respects, resembles the monastic. The hours of business and refreshment return in regular succession, being seldom interrupted by accidental intrusion; and the circle of active amusements is so contracted, that the man who happens not to possess the inestimable art of employing his leisure, must submit to suffer many solitary hours of insipid languor.'

However, there are also more agreeable descriptions of the expatriates making excursions on horse-back in the surrounding country and organising shooting parties and hunts with hawks and greyhounds. Perhaps not surprisingly the Europeans held together: 'Neither competition in trade nor the intervention of national ruptures in Europe, broke off this sociable intercourse in Syria.'

At the same time as the Russells were compiling their compendium of knowledge on Aleppo there was considerable construction activity in progress. It is a shame that they did not document the dynamic growth and embellishment of the city for this was the age when some of the finest private houses in the city were constructed. Bait Gazale, Bait Achikbache and Bait Jumblatt are all products of eighteenth-century Aleppo: town mansions, built around courtyards with fountains, that would stand out in the most sophisticated urban setting as places of refined living. Unlike the dwellings of Damascus, the houses of Aleppo are made of limestone and have weathered more gracefully.

Although the Ottomans governed Aleppo for four centuries through the person of a *wazir pasha* who ensured discipline by inflicting some gruesome forms of capital punishment – it was standard practice to send back the heads of the victims to Constantinople – the city itself appears as an authentic Arab product of the age. Its fifteen kilometres of subterranean *suqs* are as Arabian in structure and atmosphere as could be wished for. Here in the gloom, occasionally illuminated by shafts of bright sunlight, the age-old traditions of the Middle East are maintained, where the men of the desert and the farms meet those from the town. The walls and gates of Aleppo – as well as those of the Citadel – are all from the Arab period, built between the thirteenth and sixteenth centuries. The only obvious Turkish note is given by the Osman Pasha Madrasa which is a direct cultural transplant from Constantinople.

Set side by side, Aleppo and Damascus demonstrate to a remarkable degree a common historical experience, but at the same time the dichotomy imposed by geography has had a telling effect. Both cities are unmistakably Syrian, but the city in the north has been fashioned primarily by its merchant tradition whereas the one in the south has combined its trade with the pastoral enjoyment of the oasis, tempered by the close proximity of the desert. Both have an array of Islamic monuments rivalled only by Cairo and an impressive claim to be the oldest continuously inhabited city in the world. Archaeologists have yet to resolve this matter but the fact remains that together Damascus and Aleppo have experienced as much of the history of the entire Middle East, both its glories and its tragedies, as any other urban centres in the region.

A note on the transliteration of Arabic proper names

Anyone who has visited Syria will have discovered that the names he or she gives to places often do not correspond to those used by Syrians. Thus Damascus is ash-Sham and sometimes Dimashq; Aleppo is Halab; the Euphrates is al-Furat, and so on. Ancient sites usually have two very distinct names, the one historical and the other local. The Greeks and Romans introduced a whole new set of place names to Syria, some of which have been arabised, others discarded. In common English usage it is sometimes the ancient name and sometimes the Arabic name that is most current, and sometimes something in between. The following list gives those place names most often used in English texts together with their Arabic counterparts, where these are significantly different.

Aleppo	Halab
Antioch	Antakia
Apamea	Afamia/Qala'at al-Madiq
Carchemish	Jerablus
Chalcis	Qinnisrin
Chastel Blanc	Safita
Cyrrhus	Nabi Houri
Damascus	Dimashq ash-Sham
Dura Europos	Salhiye
Ebla	Tell Mardikh
Guzana	Tell Halaf
Krak des Chevaliers	Qala'at al-Hosn
Latakia	al-Ladhiqiya
Mari	Tell Hariri
Orontes	al-A'asi
Palmyra	Tadmor
Qaddesh	Tell Nebi Mend
St Simeon	Qala'at Sama'an
Ugarit	Ras Shamra

The following Greek and Latin names are occasionally used but the Arabic or English name (in the right hand column) is more commonly used in English texts.

Beroea	Aleppo
Bostra	Bosra
Emesa	Homs
Laodicea	Latakia
Philippopolis	Shahba
Sergiopolis	Resafa
Tortosa	Tartus

The names of people are generally given a direct phonetic English equivalent. The more accurate rendering of Salah al-Din has been used in order to present the reader with a name less burdened with legendary associations and with a more obvious Islamic identity. On the other hand, Ananias has been used because of its familiarity from the Bible, rather than the Arabic Hanania.

Selected further reading

Browning, Iain   *Palmyra*, Chatto & Windus, 1979

Butler, H.C.   *Early Churches in Syria*, 1929; reprinted Hakkert, Amsterdam, 1969
Ancient Architecture in Syria, Brill, Leyden, 1908–20

Creswell, K.A.C.   *Early Muslim Architecture*, Volume I (Parts I & II), Oxford, 1969

Fedden, Robin   *Syria – An Historical Appreciation*, Robert Hale, 1946

Gabrieli, Francesco   *Arab Historians of the Crusades*, Routledge and Kegan Paul, 1969

Grabar, Oleg   *The Formation of Islamic Art*, Yale University Press, 1973
City in the Desert – Qasr Al-Hayr East, Harvard University Press, 1978

Hitti, Philip K.   *History of Syria*, Macmillan, 1951

Hopkins, Clark   *The Discovery of Dura Europos*, Yale University Press, 1979

Klengel, Horst   *Art of Ancient Syria*, A.S. Barnes & Co, 1972

Maalouf, Amin   *The Crusades through Arab Eyes*, Al Saqi, 1984

Matthiae, Paolo   *Ebla, An Empire Rediscovered*, Hodder and Stoughton, 1980

Parrot, André   *Mari – Capitale Fabuleuse*, Payot, 1974

Rostovtzeff, M.   *Dura Europos and its Art*, Oxford, 1938

Runciman, Steven   *A History of the Crusades*, 3 vols, Cambridge University Press, 1951–54, and Penguin Books, 1971

Russell, Alexander & Patrick   *The Natural History of Aleppo*, London, 1794

Saadé, Gabriel   *Ougarit – Métropole Cananéenne*, 1978

Tchalenko, G.   *Villages Antiques de la Syrie du Nord*, 3 vols, 1953–8

Thubron, Colin   *Mirror to Damascus*, Heinemann, 1967

Usama ibn Murshid (Ibn Munqidh)   *An Arab-Syrian Gentleman and Warrior in the Period of the Crusades*, translated by P.K. Hitti, New York, 1929

By more than one author:

Au Pays de Baal et d'Astarté, Association Francaise d'Action Artistique, 1983

Land des Baal, Philipp von Zabern, 1982

Les Reclus Syriens & *Les Stylites Syriens*, Studium Biblicum Franciscanum, Franciscan Printing Press, 1975 and 1978

Gold shop, Aleppo suq.

Textile merchant, Aleppo suq.

Aleppo street scene (right).

Glass blowing, Aleppo.

Sharpening tools, Damascus.

Polishing a ship's screw, Arwad.

Coppersmith, Aleppo (right).

Bath house, Damascus (above).

Bath house, Aleppo (left).

Great Mosque, Aleppo.

Church at Sednaya (right).

Traditional coffee at a modern hotel, Damascus.

Traditional music at a wedding.

One of the famous 'norias' (waterwheels), Hama.

Mosque of Khalid ibn al-Walid in Homs (above).

Entrance to the Great Mosque of the Umayyads, Damascus (left).

Index

Page numbers in italics refer to illustrations.

al-A'asi *see* Orontes, river
Abbasids, 92, 93–4, 113
Abd al-Malik, caliph, 83
Abd al-Rahman, prince, 92
Abu-Bakr, caliph, 80
Abu Kemal, 5, 20
Achikbache House, Aleppo, *75*, 124
Afamia (Apamea), 19–20
Aglibol, moon god, *54*
agriculture, 23, 31, 91
    birth of, 13
Ain Dara, 16
Ain Jalut (Goliath Spring), 96, 115
Akkadians, 11
    language, 2, 10
Aleppo (Halab), 12, 45, *72–3*, *75*, 96, 119–24
    Citadel, *72*, 103, 121, 122
    contemporary, *128–30*, *131–2*, *134*
    under Hamdanids, 94
Alexander the Great, 15, 17, 19
Alexander Severus, 25
Ali, cousin to Mohammed, 82
alphabet, phonetic, 2, 17
Amorites, 6, 7, 12
Amrit (Marathus), 17–18, *49*
Ananias, house of, 33–4
Anat (daughter of El), 3
Antioch (Antakia), 19, 34, 40, 41, 44, 45, 94, 98, 99, 107, 111, 120
Apamea (Afamia), 19–20, 111
Apollinaris, Bishop of Laodicea, 44
al-Aqsab, Damascus, 115
Aram, 110
Aramaeans, 15–17, 110, 111, 113, 120
Aramaic language, 16–17, 20
Arianism, 44
Arwad (Ruad), 17, 100
Asad Pasha al-Azm, 118
asceticism, 38, 43
Ashirat (consort of El), 3
Assassins, 104
Assur, 10, 11
Assyrians, 16, 110

Augustus, emperor, 21, 23
Aurelian, emperor, 28
Ayyubids, 96, 121
Azm Palace, Damascus, *76*, 118

Baal, cycle of, 3–4
Baal, Temple of, 27, 29, *54*, 112
Babylon, 8
Baibars, Sultan, 100, 101, 117
al-Bara, 35
Barada, river, 109, 110, 111
Barada panel, *65*, 86–8, 113
basalt, black, 7, 25, 35
Belisarius, 45
Berchem, Marguerite van, 86–7, 93
Berchem, Max van, 103
Beroea *see* Aleppo
Bible, the, 12
Bimaristan Arghoun Mosque, 122
Bimaristan Nur al-Din, 114
Bimaristan al-Qaymari, 115
Bosra, 25
    Arab castle, 103
    Roman theatre, 25, *56–7*
Breasted, James Henry, 21
Brocquière, Bertrand de la, 116
Browning, Iain, 126
Buqras, 13
Burg Haydar, church at, *62*
Butler, H.C., 36, 126
Byblos, 10, 17
Byzantium, 21, 33, 34, 35, 37, 42, 44, 45, 46, 83, 87, 94, 107, 113, 120

Canaanites, 1, 2, 3–4, 6
Caracalla, 24
Carchemish, 2, 15
castles
    Crusader, 99–102
    Muslim, 103–104
Cathedral of St John, Damascus, 84
Chalcedon, Council of, 44
Chalcedonians, 44–5
Chastel Blanc (Safita), 100
Chosroes I, 45
Chosroes II, 45, 79

Christianity, 31, 33–46
Chrysostom, John, 45
churches (Dead Cities), 36–7
Citadel of Aleppo, *72*, 103, 121, 122
Citadel of Damascus, 103, 114, 115
'City of the Dead', Palmyra, 31
Constantine, emperor, 34
Constantinople, founding of, 34
Council of – *see under names*
Creswell, K.A.C., 83, 126
Crusades, 95–108
Cumont, Franz, 21

Damascus (Dimashq ash-Sham), 11, 23, *74*, *76–7*, 79, 96, 109–119
    Aramaean kingdom at, 16
    Citadel, 103, 114, 115
    contemporary, *130*, *133*, *136*
    Islamic conquest, 81
    St Paul and, 33–4
Darius, 15
Darwish Pasha, Mosque of, Damascus, 117
'Dead Cities', 35–7, *62–3*
Decapolis, 111
Deirouni, 37
Dera'a, 118
desert cities, 88–91
Dimashq ash-Sham *see* Damascus
Diocletian, emperor, 26
Dome of the Rock, Jerusalem, 83
Dossin, Georges, 8
Dura Europos (Salhiye), 19, 20–3, 27

Ebla (Tell Mardikh), 9–12, 14
Eblaites, 7, 10
Edessa, 96
Egyptians, 2
El, 3
Elagabulus, 24
Emesa (Homs), 24, 26, 81
Emesene Baal (deity), 24
Enkidu, *47*
Ephesus, Council of, 44
Euphrates, 22, 26, 27, 35, 41, 91, 119

Fatimids, 94, 113
Fedden, Robin, 98–9, 101–102, 126
Franks, the, 96–8, 104–105

Gabriel, Albert, 90
Gabrieli, Francesco, 96, 126
Gazale, Bait, 124
Ghengiz Khan, 115
Goliath Spring see Ain Jalut
Grabar, Oleg, 83, 90, 126
Great Mosque, Damascus see Umayyad Mosque
Greek period, 18–23
'Green Palace', Damascus, 83
Guzana see Tell Halaf

Habuba Kabira, 12–13
Halab see Aleppo
Halabiya, fortification at, 35, 60
Halifax, Dr William, 29
Hamdanids, 94
al-Hamidiye (suq), 118
Hammam al-Labbadiye (baths), Aleppo, 121
Hammurabi, 8
Hanabila Mosque, Salihiye, 115
Harun al-Rashid, caliph, 94
Hassaka, 9
Hauran, 23, 25–6, 35
Hellenistic period, 18–23
Heraclius, 46
Hijaz railway, Damascus, 118
Hippodamean system, 21
Hisham, caliph, 89
Hitti, P.K., 82, 92, 93, 96, 126
Hittin, 96
Hittites, 2, 12, 15, 16, 120
Holy War, 95–108
Homs see Emesa
Hopkins, Clark, 22
Hosn-Sulayman, temple at, 18
Hospitallers, Knights, 99, 100, 102, 107
Hulagu, 103, 115
Huntington, Dr, 29
Hurrian language, 2
al-Husain, shrine of, 121

Ibn Battuta, 86, 87, 103, 115–16
Ibn Jubayr, 109, 114–15
Ibn Taghri-Birdi, 116
Ikhshids, 94
Ishtar, temple of, 5
Ishtup-Ilum, ruler of Mari, 7
Islam, birth of, 79–82

Issus, battle of (333BC), 15

Jazirah, 91
Jerome, St, 43
Jerusalem, 11, 45
    Latin Kingdom of, 96–8
    sacking of (1099), 106–107
Julia Domna, 24, 111
Julia Maesa, 24
Jumblatt, Bait, 124

Kaparu of Guzana, 16
Kassioun, Mount, 109, 117
Khabour, river, 9
Khalid ibn al-Walid, 81
    mosque of, 78, 139
Khan Asad Pasha, 77, 117–18
Khan al-Gumruk, 117, 123
Khan al-Harir, 117
Khan al-Saboun, 123
Khan Suleyman, 117
Khan al-Wazir, 123
Kish, 10
Klengel, Horst, 10, 127
Kowaik, river, 119
Krak des Chevaliers, 68–9, 100–102

Lamgi-Mari, King of Mari, 5
Laodicea (al-Ladhiqiya), 19
Latin language, 24
Lawrence, T.E., 101

Maalouf, Amin, 97, 127
Ma'aloula, 46
Macedonians, 19
Madrasa al-Firdous, Aleppo, 72–3, 121
Madrasa al-Nuriya, Damascus, 114
Madrasa Zahiriya, Damascus, 115
al-Malik al-Adil, 103
Mallowan, Max, 9
Mamluks, 96, 103, 115, 117, 121–2
al-Mansur, 94
Marathus (Amrit), 17–18, 49
Mark Antony, 23, 27
Maron, St, 40
Marqab, castle of, 99–100
'martyrs of peace', 38
Marwan II, 92
Masyaf, Muslim castle of, 103–104

Matthiae, Paolo, 9, 11, 14
Mecca, 80, 82, 85, 93, 110
Medina, 80, 83, 85
Meryon, Dr, 30
Mesopotamia, 7
Milan, Edict of, 34, 38, 41
Mohammed, prophet, 79, 80, 110
Mongols, 96, 103, 115, 121, 122
monks, stylite, 39–40, 42–3
Monophysites, 44–5
mosaics, 65–7, 86–8
mosques, 86
    see also under names
Mot (death), 3
Muawiya, caliph, 82–3, 88
al-Muhallabi al-Bahnassi, 113
Muhyi al-Din Ibn Arabi, tomb of, 117
al-Muqaddasi, 84, 86, 87
murals, early, 13
    at Dura, 21
Mureybet, 13
Murphy, Capt. M.C., 20–1
Mushabak, church at, 63
Muslim period, 79–94
al-Mutanabbi, 94, 121

Nabataeans, 23, 25, 111
Naram-Sin, 11
Nassan House, Damascus, 74, 118
Nestorius, 44
Nicaea, Council of, 44
Nur al-Din, 96, 103, 114, 121

Odenath, 28
Old Syrian Period, 9
Old Testament, 12
Orontes (al-A'asi), river, 19, 23, 24, 104
Osman Pasha Madrasa, 124
Ottoman period
    Aleppo during, 122–4
    Damascus during, 117–19
Outremer, 97, 107–108
al-Outrouch Mosque, Aleppo, 122

Palace of Zimri-Lim, Mari, 7–8
'Palaeo-Canaanite' language, 10
Palestine, 3
Palmyra (Tadmor), 22, 27–31, 50–5, 112
Palmyrene Gods, Temple of the, Dura, 21
Parrot, André, 5, 6, 8, 127
Parthians, 20, 21–2, 23, 27, 91

Paul, St, 33, 34, 112
Petra, 27, 111, 112
Philip the Arab, 25
Philippopolis (Shahba), 25, 26
Philistines, 2–3
Phoenicians, 3, 17–18
phonetic alphabet, 2, 17
Poidebard, Père, 26
Pompey, 15
Posidonius of Apamea, 23–4
Protosyrian Period, 9, 12

Qaddesh (Tell Nebi Mend), 2
Qadem, 110
al-Qadi Mosque, Aleppo, 122
Qait-bay, Mamluk ruler, 117
Qala'at Sama'an, see St Simeon
Qalawun, 96, 100
Qalb Lozeh, 37
Qasr al-Hayr, 89–91
   al-Gharbi (Western), 64, 89–90
   al-Sharqi (Eastern), 90–1
Qasr Ibn Wardan (church), 35
Quran, 80, 109
Qutuz, Mamluk Sultan, 115

Ramad, excavations at, 110
Ramses II, 2
Raqqah (Rafiqa), 94
Ras Shamra (Ugarit), 1–5, 10
Resafa see Sergiopolis
Richard Coeur de Lion, 96
road-building, Roman, 26, 33
Roman Conquest, 15, 22–32
   Damascus and, 112–13
Roman Temple of Damascene
   Jupiter, 84, 112
Rostovtzeff, Michael, 22, 127
Ruad (Arwad), 17, 100
Runciman, Steven, 97, 98, 106–
   107, 108
Russell, Alexander, 122–24, 127
Russell, Patrick, 122–24, 127

Saadé, Gabriel, 127
Safita (Chastel Blanc), 99, 100
Saladin's castle (Sahyun), 70–1,
   99
Salah al-Din (Saladin), 96, 101,
   103, 106, 114, 121
Salhiye see Dura Europos
Salihiye, 115, 117
Saljuqs, 94, 98, 114
Saraoui Mosque, Aleppo, 122
Sargon of Akkad, 7, 119
Sassanians, 22, 45, 79, 91

Saul of Tarsus (St Paul), 33, 34,
   112
Sayf al-Dawla, 94, 121
Schaeffer, Claude, 1
sculpture, 6, 7, 25, 31, 55
Sea Peoples, 2, 120
Sednaya, church at, 46, 135
Seleucids, 19–20, 91
Seleucus Nicator, 19
Selim I, 117
Semites, 6–7
   language, 10
Septimius Severus, 24, 111
Sergiopolis (Resafa), 35, 41–2,
   45, 60–1
Sergius, St, 41
Shahba see Philippopolis
Shapur I, 22
Sheizar, Muslim castle of, 104
Sidon, 17
Simeon, St, 37–41, 44
   church of, 37, 41, 58–9
Sinan Pasha, Mosque of,
   Damascus, 117
Solomon's Temple, 16
'spindles' of Amrit, 18
Stanhope, Lady Hester, 30
statues, 6, 7, 25, 31
stone masonry, 7, 25, 36, 37
Strabo, 19
Straight, Street called
   (Damascus), 33, 112
Strata Diocletiana, 26
stylite movement, 39–40, 42–3
Sumer, 6
Sumerians, 5, 6
   language, 2, 10, 11

Tablets
   Ebla, 10–12
   Mari, 8
   Ugarit, 1–4
Tadmor see Palmyra
Tamerlane see Timur
Tancred, Prince of Antioch, 104
'tariff' of Palmyra, 27
Tartus see Tortosa
Tavernier, Jean-Baptiste, 29
Tchalenko, G., 127
Tekkieh of Suleiman the
   Magnificent, 117
Telanissos, monastery at, 38, 41
Tell Brak, 9
Tell Halaf (Guzana), 9, 15–16,
   47

Tell Hariri (Mari), 5–8, 10, 11
Tell Mardikh (Ebla), 9–12, 14
Tell Nebi Mend (Qaddesh), 2
Templar, Knights, 100, 102, 107
temples see under names
Thawra, 13
Theodoret, 38–9
Thubron, Colin, 127
Tiglathpileser III, 16, 110
Timur (Tamerlane), 115, 116,
   122
Tinkiz Mosque, Damascus, 115
Tortosa (Tartus), 17
   castle of, 100
   Cathedral of Our Lady, 100
Trajan, emperor, 22
Tripoli, 100, 101, 107
Tulunids, 94
Tyre, 17

Ugarit (Ras Shamra), 1–5, 10
Ugaritic language, 2
Umar, caliph, 80, 81
Umayyad caliphate, 82–93
Umayyad Mosque, Aleppo,
   120–1
Umayyad Mosque, Damascus,
   65–7, 83–8, 110, 138
Ur, Treasures of, 6
Ur-Nina, statue of, 6
Urban II, Pope, 95, 98
Uruk, 12–13
Usama ibn Munqidh, 104, 127
Uthman, caliph, 82

Vaballath, son of Zenobia, 28
Valle, Pietro della, 29
Verus, emperor, 22
Vogüé, Melchior de, 36

al-Walid, caliph, 83, 84–5
Walid II, 91–2
Wood and Dawkins, 29

Yamhad, King of, 7
Yamhad, kingdom of, 12, 120

Zahir Ghazi, 121
Zahiriya, Aleppo, 121
Zangi, Atabeg, 96, 121
Zenobia, 28–9
Zimri-Lim, 119–120
   palace of, 7–8

Nabi Houri (*Cyrrhus*)

Jerablus (*Carchemish*)

Ain Dara

Qala'at Sama'an (*St. Simeon*)

Antakia (*Antioch*)

Qalb Lozeh

Aleppo (*Beroea*)

Qinnisrin (*Chalcis*)

Tell Mardikh (*Ebla*)

Lake Ass

ath-Thaw

Ras Shamra (*Ugarit*)

Sahyun

al-Bara

Latakia (*Laodicea*)

Qala'at al-Madiq (*Apamea*)

Sheizar

Qasr Ibn Wardan

Marqab

Masyaf

Hama

Tartus (*Tortosa*)

Safita (*Chastel Blanc*)

Arwad

Amrit

Qala'at al-Hosn (*Krak des Chevaliers*)

Homs (*Emesa*)

Tadmor (*Palmyra*)

Tell Nebi Mend (*Qaddesh*)

Tripoli

al- A'asi (Orontes)

Qasr al-Hayr al-Gharbi

Baalbek

Ma'aloula

Beirut

Barada

Anti-Lebanon

Sednaya

Beqa'a Valley

Damascus (*Aram*)

Shahba (*Philippopolis*)

Hauran

Dera'a

Suweida

Bosra (*Bostra*)

Jerusalem

Amman